S0-AEH-238

OUDOLF
HUMMELO

PIET OUDOLF

NOEL KINGSBURY

OUDOLF HUMMELO

A Journey Through a Plantsman's Life

THE MONACELLI PRESS

Published in the United States in 2015
by The Monacelli Press

Library of Congress Control Number: 2014954998

Design
Gert Jan Slagter, Groningen, The Netherlands
Project coordination and editing
Hélène Lesger, Books, Rights & More, Amsterdam, The Netherlands
Text editing
Stacee Gravelle Lawrence, The Monacelli Press
Production
Wouter Eertink, Graven 13, Deventer, The Netherlands
Editorial assistance
Annelies ter Brugge, Zutphen, The Netherlands
Printing
DZS Grafik, Slovenia

www.monacellipress.com

First edition

CONTENTS

INTRODUCTION

The group of tourists looks out over the city. One takes a photograph while others point to something in the cityscape. The view down the street from two stories high, however, soon exhausts their interest and they move on. Just a few feet later, something else seizes the attention of one of the group—a flower in front of her. Soon everyone is photographing it. Progress along the elevated walkway keeps being delayed by plants, which attract their attention again and again. Meanwhile, one of the group has become separated from the others, so intent is he on taking a photograph of a witty slogan on an advertising billboard that peeks out from behind a foreground of wild grasses.

An everyday scene on the High Line in New York, one of the world's most radical experiments in urban landscape design. The decision to turn an abandoned, elevated freight line into a public park was in any case a brave decision, but what has crowned its success has been the planting that is an integral part of it. A rich assemblage of plant species designed to create a dynamic visual texture in every season draws people to the park; more than any botanic garden, it seems, the combination of design-heavy hardscape elements that encourage lingering, the narrowness of the track, and the park's bustling location have made people look at plants in a way they never have before.

The idea for the regeneration of the railway came from a citizen group, Friends of the High Line, the master plan from landscape design company James Corner Field Operations in cooperation with Diller Scofidio + Renfro. The planting on the High Line, however, is very much part of its global reputation. It was created by Dutch garden and landscape designer Piet Oudolf, now undoubtedly the most famous member of his profession. His work, which is primarily in public spaces, has brought plants to people in cities a new way, and highlights how effective planting design can be in creating enriching, memorable spaces. In a world where over half the population now lives in urban areas, and where nature seems in full retreat in the face of humanity's urge to reshape the planet for its own ends, the creation of beautiful, biodiverse, and ever-changing plantings is perhaps one of the keys to our future sanity and ability to share our space with other living things. This volume is about Piet and his work, but it is not a biography, for reasons we shall see later. He is the most successful and gifted contemporary exponent of a movement in planting design, but understanding what he does involves understanding the movement as a whole. So although it focuses on Piet Oudolf, his story is told very much in the context of the new planting.

To introduce our subject, I shall introduce Piet and his family, and then say a little more about contemporary planting design and the personalities who have shaped it.

Brief Biography

This book was written to mark Piet's seventieth birthday. Born on October 27, 1944, he was brought up in Bloemendaal, a town in the sand dune country near the city of Haarlem, just west of Amsterdam. His family ran a restaurant and bar. "It was" he says, "only a kilometer from Thijsse's Hof, a small *heempark*, or wild flora park, where we liked to go to when we were children, but at that time I did not understand its importance." As a young man, Petrus (to give him his full name) helped out in the business of course, but soon developed an interest in garden-making. He says that "the interest started when I was around twenty-five years of age, after having made the decision not to stay in the family business." I remember him once showing me the house where he lived as a young man, in a neighborhood of Haarlem, and pointing out a large bamboo's lush green foliage poking out above a fence—he told me it was one of the first things he ever planted. He went on to study landscape construction, which gave him the qualifications needed to set up a garden-building company. Although he started off doing all of the work himself, he soon began to bring in other skilled craftsmen to do the hard landscaping, as he wanted to concentrate on planting. As with many who fall in love with the incredible diversity of plants that can be so easily grown in our mild and moist corner of Europe, he soon found himself needing more space. So he and his family moved to the outskirts of the village of Hummelo, which is where we shall in due course begin our story.

Piet is very much a family man. Anyone who has any dealings with him soon meets his wife Anja, whose support has been a crucial part of his working life. The two of them are clearly very close and very fond of each other. "Anja takes care of me and runs a lot of things I cannot run," says Piet. "She is the social part of what I do; she is the communicator and so we are complementary." Their son Pieter lives in a nearby town and drops in frequently. He has his father's passion for design, manifested in a business selling reproduction Delft and contemporary tiles. Another son, Hugo, lives in rural Ecuador in his wife's village and has three children.

Piet looks classically Dutch—tall with blond hair and the tanned face of someone who has spent a lot of time outside. With a shyness that sometimes gets mistaken for aloofness, he tends to be a man of few words. I have always imagined him as a sea captain of the Dutch East India Company (the VOC) that played such an important part in Dutch history, his eyes set on the far horizon, braving whatever weather came his way. Once you get to know him, you realize he has a great deal of personal warmth and a strong desire to connect. Private garden design is a curiously social profession; it inevitably involves repeat meetings with clients, dealings with their families, and usually several meals. Piet seems particularly good at forging real friendships with clients as well as with collaborators on projects.

Fame notoriously corrupts, yet everyone who knows him will assure you that Piet has not altered his temperament at all. "He doesn't change in the company of high-profile people," says Joyce Huisman, a friend of some thirty years. "He is a fabulous model of collaboration, he looks and listens ... a prince of a guy," says U.S. colleague Rick Darke. Piet is actually distinctly unimpressed by other people's fame, so is perhaps unlikely to see himself on a pedestal either. His modesty is also a very typical Dutch characteristic. This is the nation whose wealthiest citizens chose sober black clothes

JAC P. THIJSSE AND HEEMPARKS

The Netherlands may be the world's most artificially "constructed" country, but it now features an unprecedented amount of re-created nature. In part this is the legacy of Jacobus Pieter Thijsse (1865–1945), usually referred to as Jac Thijsse. He was born some five years before the last area of original Dutch forest was felled during an era of intensive land reclamation that saw vast areas of heathland and forest turned into agricultural land—much more than the widely-publicized reclamation of marshland or open water.

Thijsse was a schoolteacher who became a passionate exponent of conservation and the use of nature as a means of teaching biology and natural history. Along with another teacher colleague, Eli Heimans, he wrote the first popular Dutch flora, produced teaching materials for schools and youth groups, and campaigned for both preservation and the creation of new places for wildlife.

One aspect of Thijsse's work, and likewise of the *heempark* (habitat park) movement today, is that a dogmatic "natives only" approach was never adopted. Thijsse accepted a certain number of naturalized aliens, in contrast to the 'Nordic' gardens of Willy Lange over the German border.

Toward the end of his life, Thijsse's work resulted in the creation of the first *heemparks,* a public space designed as a park and planted with native species. In the town of Amstelveen, which at the time was being laid out as a new suburb of the ever-expanding Amsterdam, two *heemparks* were created by C.P. Broerse, a landscape designer who had made it his life's work to build natural-style environments, and who had become the director of local parks. The community of Amstelveen went on to become one of the most advanced models of the integration of urban environments and nature anywhere, where "green is a total system, green is a coinhabitant, we bring it to the front door of the citizens," in the words of retired parks director Hein Koningen.

Broerse, who coined the term *heempark*, believed that naturalistic parks and gardens should first be as beautiful as possible. They were never intended to be scientifically accurate recreations of native plant communities. He took native habitats—woodlands, bogs, dunes, meadows, heaths—as his starting point and aimed to distill the essence of their character while maximizing their aesthetic appeal. He achieved this by taking a pictorial view of his selected native plant communities, selecting a limited number of key "character species" that defined their visual appeal, and using them in greater numbers than might be found in

Jac. P. Thijsse.
As a child, Oudolf lived only a few hundred meters away from the gardens at Thijsse's Hof, in Bloemendaal, The Netherlands, which commemorates Jac Thijsse's work with native plants and natural topography.

the wild. Much emphasis was placed on creating a rich herbaceous layer as well as establishing an overall framework of trees and shrubs.

Broerse's legacy continued with Hein Koningen, a young nurseryman with a passion for native flora. He joined the municipal workforce at a junior level, eventually becoming the supervisor of all the Amstelveen *heemparks*, and retiring from that position in 2001. Hein became very much a part of the Dutch Wave movement, and the management techniques he had refined from Broerse's original work were frequently studied and written about by Dutch, British, German, and Swedish colleagues. Central to his management philosophy is exploitation of the process of succession, whereby once land is cleared one plant community succeeds another until a mature forest is achieved. In Amstelveen parks, this process is managed for aesthetic interest to create a patchwork of habitats. The results are some very special landscapes.

at a time when everywhere else jewelled and embroidered opulence was essential to impress—just look at Rembrandt's 1662 painting *The Wardens of the Amsterdam Drapers' Guild.* This modesty based in Calvinism is why this book is not a biography, a literary form the Dutch have never easily indulged. "Only footballers have biographies written about them," says Piet rather disdainfully. Along with modesty comes an openness to people and a willingness to listen. It has a practical side as well. If you want your creations to be cherished and kept looking good, you need to get on well with the maintenance staff—a relative egalitarianism is another very Dutch characteristic.

Above all, Piet loves the fact that his work brings joy to so many people. This is one reason he prefers public spaces over private gardens. To work, a garden has to be looked after. Warrie Price, who commissioned him to create a series of plantings for Battery Park in New York, says that "Piet is very aware that he does not want to make a garden for a place or a group that he thinks will not maintain what he does." Gardens are not one-off creations; Piet always wants to be involved in overseeing their ongoing management. Sometimes of course, this does not happen.

Planting Design

The creative process of putting plants together for decorative or even functional purposes has historically been a rather underrated skill. As a clearly articulated art form, it probably reached a high point in early-twentieth-century Germany, but it is a field with few stars: the English Gertrude Jekyll (1843–1932) and the Brazilian Roberto Burle Marx (1909–1994) are two of the names posterity will easily remember. It will perhaps be one of Piet's most important legacies that he has done so much to raise the profile of landscape designers as a group.

Piet is part of a new movement in planting design that has ecological considerations at its base, and this book focuses very much on him in that context. The movement itself is not rigidly defined—he is simply the most successful of many like-minded practitioners. There is no manifesto, no membership, and it remains open, fluid, and welcoming. I consider myself very much part of this movement too.

I research, write, and work as a planting design consultant and I have known Piet since 1994, so writing this has at times felt like writing a personal memoir.

This movement has always stressed the importance of a deep knowledge of plants and an appreciation of plant diversity. From the 1980s onward, a growing number of professionals and amateurs in Europe —primarily in Germany, The Netherlands, Sweden, and Britain—have been developing new planting styles. In full revolt against the formulaic use of plants, as manifested either in summer beds full of annuals that have changed little since the nineteenth century or in dull "green cement" shrub planting as used en masse by the landscape industry beginning in the 1960s, many practitioners now feel an intense desire to create landscapes in a looser, more romantic, and above all more natural style. The sense of this new planting as being in defiance of historical landscape practices is key.

Various labels have been attached to this new look in planting. British commentators have referred to the "Dutch Wave," but this idea has been a controversial one. The "New Perennial Style" has also been used, after the title of a book I wrote in 1996. Recently we have also been hearing mention of the "New German Style" too, with reference to the very distinctive perennial style that has evolved in that country since the 1980s. Each of these distinct garden cultures has developed its own characteristics, but underlying them all are the same three tenets: a strong desire for a naturalistic aesthetic, sustainability, and a focus on creating a home for biodiversity.

Magazine and newspaper editors like to be able to name movements—it makes them definable and easily recognizable for readers. They also like leaders. Unless they are editing a garden publication, they also tend to have little grasp of current trends in the garden world. This can make for a lot of misunderstandings. Piet is often portrayed, therefore, as a leader of an ecological planting movement. While ecology is an important aspect of his work, it is actually not the most important. There are very definitely common goals shared by the current wave of designers working with perennials, and the desire to be inspired by nature is at the core of what we all do, but it is too varied a movement to be defined by a single manifesto.

Some very successful designers get stuck in a rut because they find a set of ideas that work and that everyone likes—particularly clients. Many designers are capable of working in different styles or moods but do not move on because clients so often request what they have seen created for others. One thinks of Louis XIV eyeing up the unfortunate Nicolas Fouquet's garden at Vaux le Vicomte, thinking how much he would like to employ Le Nôtre to make something even bigger and better! (For those who do not know the story, Fouquet ended up in jail for the rest of his life and Le Nôtre was set to work building the gardens at Versailles.)

Piet has stated that he does not like to have to repeat himself. That he is always moving forward, experimenting, trying new combinations, new ways of distributing plants, and different viewpoints makes his work exciting, but I suspect it can also sometimes unnerve clients. His design always takes into account the site conditions, the surrounding landscape, whether the garden is public or private, etc., but essentially each project becomes a chapter in a story, a unique composition that reflects everything he has learned to date about plants and planting—and is therefore necessarily different from anything he has done before. The same site, if the roulette wheel of history were to be replayed, would probably have received a different treatment if it had been developed a few years previously, or if it were to be presented to him a few years later. It is worth pointing out, however, that Piet's new design techniques tend to be cumulative. He will not abandon a particular way of putting plants together per se, but in a new project will use several new techniques. The result is a multilayered, complex composition and an increasing ability to fine-tune design solutions for particular visual and ecological environments. As he puts it, "knowledge creates freedom!"

Piet works, as do many artists, in a highly visual and intuitive way. This can make it singularly difficult to record the heart of his methodology. He has very few fixed ways of working, which can be frustrating for students. I remember him explaining once to a multinational group that sometimes he starts designing a garden with one category of plants, and sometimes with another—there were puzzled faces. There is no predictable path in his design method. This is probably one reason why each of his landscapes is so creative, and explains somewhat why he is able to achieve so many different effects with his preferred palette of plants. It does pose difficulties for those wanting to learn from him. Students like rules. They want bullet points, tips, clear procedures. "Breaking the rules" is a phrase that Piet uses often. My role in documenting his work here, I suppose, is to introduce the reader to some rules, to present them in an understandable way, and to then encourage them to be broken. These lessons, therefore, are not intended as dogma.

Noel Kingsbury

HUMMELO, THE BEGINNING

In 1982 Piet and Anja and their two boys—Pieter, then aged nine, and Hugo, aged seven—moved into an old farmhouse on an acre of land outside the village of Hummelo, in the province of Gelderland in the eastern Netherlands. The move was about space, land, and the opportunity to grow. As Piet says, "we were living in the suburbs, with a small garden, and I was having to trial plants in my mother's garden … I was working in circles, doing small garden design. I had a nice number of clients, but felt I wanted to do more … this was a step toward the life we wanted."

Having built up a successful garden design and construction practice in the Haarlem area, Piet was becoming increasingly interested in plants. He saw the enormous potential of perennials and grasses in garden design, but was frustrated at not being able to buy them from nurseries; even if he could only small quantities would be available, and not at wholesale prices. A book by veteran garden and landscape designer Mien Ruys made a strong impact on him, and helped to awaken what he describes as "a healthy obsession" with perennials. *Het Vaste Plantenboek* (*The Perennial Plant Book*), published in 1950 and held in high regard for many years afterward, was an important source of inspiration and reference for Piet. He felt certain that the type of adventurous planting he wanted to pursue had great potential, but without a source of plants it would be impossible to make any progress. He therefore decided to set up his own nursery.

Like anyone who gets excited about plants knows, space to grow them soon becomes an issue. Living in Haarlem was beginning to feel like being fenced in. Piet's creativity as a designer was increasingly limited by the available space, and his development as an entrepreneur stalled.

The Plate family garden in Haarlem, The Netherlands,
one of Oudolf's earliest garden designs.

Piet had started traveling, looking for plants to try out. If he liked them, he would propagate them and use them in clients' gardens. Initially of course he looked throughout The Netherlands, but at the time there were few nurseries that offered much of a selection. Germany and England beckoned as better sources. But first, he had to have space to grow them.

From the 1970s onward, there had been a drift of idealistic young families moving from the cities to the countryside in The Netherlands, in Britain, and in other Western European countries. For Piet however, "it was not really about living in the countryside, but about growing space." The purchase of an old farmhouse on just over three acres (13,000 square meters) offered a new beginning. Initially, though, there was an enormous amount of work to do. "The house was completely derelict, with tiles coming off the roof," he recalls. "I did all the building work, the fitting in the house, the plastering, roofing—it was constant work but I had experience. I had already renovated two houses in Haarlem."

Initially, Piet was in partnership with Romke van de Kaa, who had worked for renowned English gardener and writer Christopher Lloyd as head gardener (a very valuable contact), and then in Ireland. "We met at a magazine-sponsored meeting," Piet recollects. "I had realized I could not do everything on my own, so I needed a partner." Romke stayed until 1985. "We developed in separate ways," Piet says. "He was more an intellectual, a connoisseur, he had started to write ... I was working hard to do the physical work. In the end he started his own nursery in Dieren, a town nearby." Although the partnership did not continue, Piet emphasises that, "Romke showed me the way to English gardens and nurseries." This, it turns out, was absolutely crucial to his development as a plantsman, as a grower, and as a designer.

The first few years on the new property were challenging. "We had cashed in a mortgage, and had money to survive one year ... and at first we had no clients," Piet says, the implication being that poverty was not far off. He remembers that they underestimated the work needed on the house. "I was working on the house at night, building the nursery in the day." Initially, their only source of income was Anja's cut-flower business. Local flower shops began to fill with plants many customers had never seen before: astrantias, echinaceas, eryngiums, even delicate

Family life revolved around making improvements to the property and the nursery in the earliest days at Hummelo.

Frosted winter landscapes have always resonated with Piet.

sprays of *Gillenia trifoliata*. "It was a big change, coming to Hummelo," Anja recalls. "It was not always easy here, there was no heating in the hard winters … we had a wood stove and when it was very cold, we would get up twice a night to keep it going. But we just looked forward, kept looking forward all the time."

Pieter remembers that the move to Hummelo happened when "I was young enough for it to seem playful … it was different. There were farms, the fields, the farmers' children in the school." He recalls that his father worked on the house for months before they moved in as a family. There was plenty of space and many opportunities for the boys to play. "I remember we built a tree house and later had a little moped to ride around the countryside … I kept pet salamanders and frogs." Later on, the boys helped a little on the nursery and also worked for a landscape contractor nearby. Pieter remembers having to help with watering because they did not have an automatic system. When he was about twenty he started to grow his own box trees, keeping them clipped so that they could be sold as mature specimens to garden designers. He still has a field locally, and continues to sell them.

Anja looked after the house and the boys, and says that "I didn't get involved when Piet was working with Romke, but after he left I got a lot more involved in the plants. I learned about the species and how to grow them." This is her modest way of saying that she started to run the nursery. As the nursery expanded, she had to oversee the annual round of propagation, potting, setting out into the sales area, and of course dealing with customers. The nursery soon developed a retail life of its own, with people coming to buy plants from far and wide. Anja took up the role of "front of house" with enthusiasm, greeting visitors and potential customers, serving them, making coffee for those who stayed longer. She is naturally outgoing, so her role as the public face for the business became invaluable, although of course she was also a behind-the-scenes organizer. Running the nursery, to say nothing of the numerous events that were held there, involved a lot of personnel management. She brought in local women to help propagate, make coffee, provide food and serve customers. Anja made it all run smoothly. Practically everyone who has told me about their visits to Hummelo soon mentions Anja and her cheerful and efficient style. For her, it was a perfect combination, "I was always happy with the mix: the people, the plants, and being out in the open."

The Garden: Taking the First Steps

Initially there was no garden as such. The soil varied enormously across the property, but was generally a loamy sand, good and fertile for growing plants and not too heavy, although there were some patches of clay. Behind the house there was an area that had held sheds and outbuildings; these were cleared and a nursery area for containerized plants was laid out with concrete edgings and paths. Sand was brought in to ensure good drainage. Two small rectangular ponds were also made, but they leaked and so were taken out. Piet recalls that he "later made a round pond in the front, although it was not really meant to be a pond at first … it was dug to collect water after heavy rainfall in the winter." Photographs from the time show the land around the house as completely open, with only one short run of beech hedging. The space at the very back, behind the nursery area, was taken up with beds for trial plants, mother plants to propagate from, and rows of perennials being grown on.

In 1986 more beds for trial and stock plants were made at the front. Around this time too, Piet and Anja were able to complete a property deal with a neighbor that allowed them to buy some land adjacent to their lot, which gave them space for a longer drive and an area on which to erect a greenhouse and make additional growing space. Negotiations had dragged on for a few years, so the resolution, which involved swapping some land, came as a considerable relief.

Much of the area at the front of the house was laid out for trial beds of perennials. A block of yew was also planted, for growing on for use as good-sized transplants into clients' gardens. Piet took out alternate rows and was left with a quantity that was not immediately needed, so he had an idea—why not leave them and shape them into hedges? The distinctive forms that resulted became a decorative feature in their own right and one of the most famous parts of the garden at Hummelo, until their demise as the result of flooding in 2011. As a backdrop the sculptural hedges worked supremely well, a culmination of the build-up created by the yew columns that beat a rhythm through the lawn and borders of the garden.

Many of the trial and mother plants in the nursery came from England, which the more adventurous Dutch gardeners of the time saw as the best source for interesting plants. Traveling at first with Romke, who knew the southeastern counties of Kent and Sussex from his years

Early pictures of the front garden and future nursery.

Against the backdrop of Hummelo's agricultural landscape,
the nursery begins to take shape.

Piet constructs the garden's early greenhouses, while Anja gathers plants at Washfield nursery.

working at Great Dixter with Christopher Lloyd, Piet found the range and availability of plants a revelation. One of Romke's introductions was to Elizabeth Strangman, who had a specialist nursery—Washfield.

Washfield had existed since the early 1950s and by the time Piet first visited in 1982, was run by Mrs. Strangman, who made her name partly through her hellebores, a plant that was beginning to develop almost cult status. She had traveled and collected plants in the Balkans, there discovering some natural double hellebores in the wild that she then used in a breeding program. Using basic hybridization techniques, she produced a range of hellebores that effectively launched the modern interest in the plant. Her nursery manager was Graham Gough, who, after sixteen years working at Washfield, went on to establish his own business, Marchants Hardy Plants. His nursery was famous for its garden as much as for its innovative range of perennials.

Other places Piet visited and bought plants from include Blackthorn Nursery—where Robin White was also working on hellebores—and of course Beth Chatto's nursery and display garden in Essex, where her ideas about plant selection for different garden habitats was beginning to introduce British gardeners to a more ecological way of thinking. At the time, moving plants from one country to another was prohibited without plant health certification, but as customs inspections gradually became more relaxed, plant enthusiasts regularly began to fill their cars with plants and drive across borders.

MIEN RUYS

Back in the 1990s, I remember several conversations with Piet in which he would say "everything in garden design was Mien Ruys." Wilhelmina Jacoba Moussault-Ruys (1904–1999) was the most renowned garden and landscape designer of the post-war period in The Netherlands. Her career was long, influential, and varied. There is little written about her in English, but anyone seeking to understand her can visit her garden at Dedemsvaart—the Mien Ruys Tuin. No other designer's own garden reveals so much. She started gardening in her late teens on property that was part of the Royal Moerheim Nurseries, which were run by her father. This was one of the great perennial nurseries of Europe, and she continued to be involved with its affairs until her death at the age of ninety-six.

When I first visited the Mien Ruys Tuin in about 2000, I could see immediately how it had influenced Piet—although, in fact, he was soon to move on in his design work, increasingly leaving Mien Ruys behind. I could also see what we in Britain, with our fixation on the Arts and Crafts garden and our rather craven attitude to aristocratic country house gardens, had missed out on: modernism in garden design. What the visitor appreciates in the Mien Ruys Tuin is the graphic, architectural clarity of her visual imagination and her adventurous and inventive use of plants. Divided into some twenty-eight areas, the garden maps out a lifetime of creative imagination. With Ruys's father running a perennial nursery, it comes as no surprise that the young designer worked primarily with perennials, and mostly in private gardens. Apprenticed to a landscape company in England in 1927, she met the elderly Gertrude Jekyll. Later, she studied in Germany at a college in Dahlem, Berlin, where she would have been exposed to the ideas of Karl Foerster, which were on the naturalistic side. Back home in Delft, she came under the sway of the Bauhaus movement, and its focus on clean lines was to stay with her for the rest of her life.

After the war, there was of course comparatively little call for private garden design in Europe. Her strongly socialist politics, though, were very much in tune with the zeitgeist. This was the time of planning, of the design of huge areas of public housing and public facilities. Much of her work then centered on the creation of communal gardens and other public areas. Inspired by the artist Piet Mondrian and the Canadian architect and landscape designer Christopher Tunnard, her designs were graphic, asymmetric, and favored "bishop's move" oblique paths and axes. Experimenting with new materials—concrete, prefabricated slabs, and railway ties—gave her work a look that broke uncompromisingly with the past and identified with the output of modern industry. She incorporated inexpensive, mass-produced, and democratic elements.

Mien Ruys, circa 1975.

Ruys's planting design was highly experimental. She tried out a wide variety of woody plants as material for hedging or for abstract blocks, and popularized plants with chunky or textural qualities such as *Phlomis russeliana, Vitis coignetiae,* and grasses. She also founded a quarterly magazine in 1954, *Onze eigen tuin*, which is still thriving today.

Views of two of the thirty garden areas within the Mien Ruys Gardens in Dedemsvaart, which were founded in 1924 and are still open to the public today.

Dutch Gardening Goes Rural

The Netherlands is a small country, its population center in a narrow coastal strip from Amsterdam down to Rotterdam. The view of many of the inhabitants of this densely populated area is that anything farther away than an hour is very far away indeed. This was brought home to me one day when I returned to Amsterdam from a visit to the Oudolfs, and I met with Hélène Lesger, our publisher, who exclaimed something about my having returned "from the distant land of Hummelo."

The Oudolfs moved from the city to the countryside at a time when many young families were doing the same. Although their motives were driven by practical considerations—to have enough space to start a nursery—others moved as part of a trend established in the 1970s, originally rooted in the counterculture movement of the 1960s. Whereas many moved to the northern provinces, the Oudolfs were not interested in going quite so far away. Hummelo is about an hour and a half by car or train from Amsterdam, half an hour from the city of Arnhem, and an hour from the edge of the Ruhrgebiet, one of the most densely populated parts of Germany. A major recreation zone, the national park of Hoge Veluwe, is nearby. Hummelo is quiet and rural without being remote.

A key role in the Dutch Wave planting movement was played by a generation of gardeners who had gone farther out, to the north of the country two hours from Amsterdam, and, crucially, had been part of the counterculture movement. Piet, I learned early on, had never identified himself with them—he had never been a hippie. Many of his colleagues and the Dutch Wave movement as a whole, however, had been greatly influenced by counterculture thought.

The counterculture movement of the 1960s and early 1970s had of course had a major impact on all Western, industrialized countries. In The Netherlands, it played a crucial role in breaking down the traditional boundaries within a very divided and conservative society. Until then, people had been identified primarily by their religious views—Catholic, Protestant, or secular—and the different groups had had little to do with each other. The youth revolt of the sixties and seventies in all its exuberant, colorful, and occasionally violent forms was in part a rejection of this division. Protests took different political and social forms, including the squatting movement in Amsterdam and the development of a drug culture. The latter was the most radical legacy, although not the most important, which was perhaps the artistic. An anarchist group called the Provos were the noisy core of the movement, and proposed a series of measures to upend the concept of private property. Their white bicycles, which anyone could borrow and then leave on the street when they had finished with them, were the best-known expression of their rejection of "bourgeois" property.

As with counterculture movements in other countries, the latter phase was marked by a rejection of city life in favor of the country. As the youth who had participated in the movements of the 1960s began to settle down and have children of their own, they turned to rural surroundings. In the early eighties, somewhat derelict farmhouses could be purchased very cheaply. "Self-sufficiency was the fashion at the time," says Fleur van Zonneveld, who moved to the northern province of Groningen with her husband, Eric Spruit, in 1971, and started her first garden. "I purchased an old farmhouse myself and planted vegetables and fruit at first, but then we got bored with them and started growing flowers." A friend, Rob Leopold, had also moved up north and was particularly interested in plants and gardening; he went on to become the key figure in the Dutch Wave. Leopold had studied philosophy at university with Eric in the late sixties, and had lived on a commune in Leiden. "Rob had some pretty wild friends," recalls Leo den Dulk, another long-standing member of the Dutch Wave garden scene. Fleur recalls that the experimentation with hallucinogens had already been left behind by the time they all moved, but their youthful energy and rebelliousness drove them to look for new outlets for self-expression. One was gardening, another was nature.

Many sixties radicals and rebels joined the nascent "green" movement, particularly those who lived in the cities; those already in the country drifted naturally toward farming and gardening. During this period the Dutch countryside was being increasingly industrialized. Due to growing population pressure and rising incomes, demand for agricultural produce soared, pushing farmers to adopt measures that allowed for greater efficiencies. These often resulted in the destruction of wildflower-rich habitats like meadows and wetlands, and nitrogen and phosphorus run-off from fertilizers polluted waterways and fueled the growth of reeds and grasses that eventually displaced other species.

Henk Gerritsen's and Anton Schlepers' garden in Priona, in the province of Overijssel.

"I remember cycling around outside Utrecht in the early 1960s," said Henk Gerritsen, "and seeing ditches filled with marsh lousewort and fields overgrown with sun spurge and scarlet pimpernel ... but they have all gone now." For Henk and many others, there was a strong desire to both conserve and to actively promote natural landscapes. In particular, a concern for the environment and a desire to garden coalesced into a growing interest in native plants and their cultivation.

For some years Henk and his partner, Anton Schlepers, divided their time between environmental campaigns in Amsterdam and Priona, a property on Anton's family farm in the sparsely populated eastern province of Overijssel, where they started making a garden in 1978. In 1983 they decided to leave the city permanently for their garden—and to flee, as Henk put it, "the fact that so many of our friends were dying from AIDS. We hoped to escape the same fate." He talks vividly about how many of his circle saw the city, and urban living, as a lost cause.

The Dutch city was, however, anything but lost. A great many people at this time were beginning to develop a more direct engagement with nature. Much was achieved through an organization called Oase (Oasis), which was officially founded in 1993, although it had already been working as an informal network for several years. The key people were a couple, Willy Leufgen and Marianne van Lier, who, also from that year onward, formed part of a collective of artists, musicians, and other creative souls who lived in a former monastery in Gelderland. Since then, Oase has run workshops, meetings, excursions, and published a quarterly journal for professionals and amateurs involved in gardening in harmony with nature. Native species have also been key to Oase, since it is primarily concerned with bringing people closer to nature through direct contact with natural environments, gardening, and art. "One of our love babies," as Willy put it, "has been Elyseum, a training course for ecological gardening, which has helped educate many thousands in the art and practice of nature-inspired garden making."

Revival in the North

Many of the generation of young idealists who moved out of the cities in the seventies went north, to the three provinces of Friesland, Groningen, and Drenthe. Fleur van Zonneveld and Eric Spruit were among them, as were Rob Leopold and his wife Ans, known as Ansje. Rob and Ansje set up a shop in Groningen selling imported, handcrafted goods from Nepal and Afghanistan, and eventually moved out to a cottage in the countryside. There, Rob created a vast trial field of annuals and perennials. With them went others who, although perhaps not a part of the counterculture movement, were seeking open skies, uncrowded roads, and, crucially, low property prices. Today, the north is populated by many artists as well as garden-makers and small growers. It is still a place that attracts creative souls, and the area reflects their energy.

The tendency of Amsterdammers and others who live in the coastal cities of Holland to see the rest of the country as remote has been noted. The north is equated with being particularly isolated, especially to those from outside the country. A map reveals that it is not really on the way *to* anywhere—beyond lies the North Sea, and to the east lie the comparatively empty fields of the German province of Ostfriesland. This remoteness, however, has directly played an important role in stimulating much good new garden-making.

The 1970s and early 1980s were, by all accounts, a dull time for Dutch gardening. Just as farming was beginning to be consolidated by large industrial companies, so was commercial horticulture. Nurseries were growing ever more efficient, and producing only plants that were easy to mass produce, often for export to the rest of Europe. Perennials had fallen distinctly out of fashion. "There were only conifers, some shrubs, and stiff annuals," notes Fleur. "Very few growers were doing anything interesting. One of the few was the nursery of Mien Ruys at the Moerheim, and also Ploeger ... commercial nurseries only offered a narrow range of plants, so people would share plants with friends and neighbors." Piet recalls Kwekerij De Bloemenhoek, run by Herman van Beusekom as "one of my first treasure nurseries in Holland—next to Ploeger and some in Boskoop—at a time when there were hardly any interesting plants." He also remembers "Heilien Tonckens with her Wilde Planten nursery promoting native plants and *stinze* plants."[1]

ROB LEOPOLD: PHILOSPHER-GARDENER

"We are in a meadow of many beautiful flowers," says a stocky man with tousled hair and arms opened expansively wide. At the moment he uttered this phrase, he was in a conference room, so it was immediately understood that the meadows of wildflowers were not literal—he was referring to the people around him, the other attendees.

This was Rob Leopold (1942–2005). He was a very good friend of Piet and Anja, and a key figure in the emerging planting movement. The sentence above is very typical of how he often spoke elliptically. He was endowed with a gift particular to some non-English speakers: the ability to convey exactly what they mean even if ungrammatical or expressing themselves in otherwise formally incorrect terms. Technical imperfections grant what they say a certain poetry denied to native speakers.

Rob was a man of many talents. He was intimately involved with the gardening world, and indeed should be counted as one of the greatest innovators of the late twentieth century—it is him we have to thank for the incredible annual meadows that are beginning to creep across urban spaces throughout Europe. It is not, however, as a technical innovator that he is remembered, but as a philosopher and networker. As Piet recalls, "Rob's ultimate strength lay in his ability to play the role of catalyst, to encourage people to discuss and think about their activities, and to find new opportunities."

Gardening became a key part of Rob's philosophy. Gardening as he saw it was partly about defining a new world vision that integrated culture and nature. He, as with many of his generation, reacted against what he described as "universalizing modernism," which manifested itself in tower-block housing, highway-centered town planning, and industrial-scale agriculture. The loss of wildflowers, of native vegetation, and of traditional landscapes affected him very deeply. It is not surprising that his interest in gardening started with growing Dutch native wildflowers.

Rob talked in philosophical terms most of the time. He was no self-centered guru figure though, quite the opposite: he was incredibly open to new experiences, people, and ideas. He became a central figure in the rapidly developing Dutch garden world of the 1980s and 1990s, was an attendee at many gardening conferences and meetings, and was always ready to introduce people to each

Piet with Rob Leopold, left, and a cover from the seed company Leopold ran with Dick van den Burg, right.

other. Bringing people together was central to his mission in life, and he saw distributing plants and seeds along with contact details as two ways to fulfill the same mission.

Rob's practical contribution to the gardening world was Cruydt-Hoeck, a seed company he set up in 1978 with another resident of Groningen province, Dick van den Burg. Their remarkable seed catalog, the *Dikke Zadenlijst*, written by Rob, contained such informative detail, its text and illustrations so much a combination of learning and enthusiasm, that it became a book rather than just a listing of items for sale. It was very much a part of its time; gardeners all over the industrialized world were then beginning to rediscover forgotten varieties of annual flowers, heritage varieties, and wild species.

Rob combined the concepts of traditional annual gardening and gardening with wildflowers by creating seed mixtures that contained annuals and wildflowers, and selling them in small packets for home gardeners. These mixes inspired an academic from England's University of Sheffield, Nigel Dunnett, to try something similar, but on a much larger scale. His resulting Pictorial Meadows seed mixes have become one of the most successful experiments of the whole period, and have stimulated practitioners in other countries to experiment even further.

Fleur van Zonneveld, top, and Henk Gerritsen and Anton Schlepers
with Elisabeth de Lestrieux, below.

“We have a very positive attitude to gardening here in the north,” notes Fleur. “We have a strong culture of women joining garden clubs and opening gardens.” The garden club movement spread rapidly in the late 1970s and early 1980s, helping to create a market for a wider range of plants. Fleur started her own nursery, de Kleine Plantage, in 1983. About the same time, an open garden movement also started. Fleur recalls that “some famous gardens began to open to the public in Limburg, in Zeeland—two southern provinces. They were run by people who traveled to England a lot, so most of their plants came from England.”

An informal group of northern gardeners, growers, and landscape architects began to form in this era. One of their first goals was to make it easier to distribute plants. In 1983 a plant fair was held at Hortus Haren, a botanical garden just south of Groningen. The Hortus Haren fairs continued for some years, helping many small nurseries find an outlet. Another development was the founding of a group in 1998 to promote garden opening in the area, in collaboration with gardeners on the other side of the border in Germany. Het Tuinpad Op (In Nachbars Garten in German)[2] organizes and publicizes open gardens in German Ostfriesland and Dutch Groningen and Drenthe. Since 2006 it has published a bilingual guide and website. “This was a new phenomenon, to look into each other’s gardens,” notes Fleur. She sees it as incentive for people to work in their gardens so they can be exhibited at their best.

During this period, the only garden that seemed to inspire interest among the younger generation was that of Mien Ruys, at Dedemsvaart, in Overijssel, although some thought it as rather old-fashioned, “the kind of garden your parents would have,” in Fleur’s words. For Henk Gerritsen though, his first visit was something of a Damascene occasion. As he once explained to me, “in 1976 I first visited the Mien Ruys garden ... although I did not like everything I saw there, it was an Ah! Ha! experience. At that time I was struggling to survive as a painter, and I suddenly realized that by gardening I could combine my artistic abilities in design, painting, and writing with my passion for nature ... two years later I started gardening at Priona.” Tuin Priona is less than ten kilometers away from Dedemsvaart, so Henk and Anton and their visitors could make frequent visits.

In 1970 another painter began to make a big, colorful impact on the Dutch garden world. Ton ter Linden started making a garden at Ruinen in Drenthe with his then-partner, Anne van Dalen. His work was given a lot of publicity by photographer Marijke Heuff, who around that time began to specialize in gardens. Ton himself made and sold many watercolors and pastels of the garden and the plants that grew in it. By 1999 over 15,000 visitors were coming annually to see his work, which blended naturalism with strong color theming. Since then, he has lived and worked with artist and photographer Gert Tabak at two other gardens, first in Limburg, and then in Friesland. His current home is at the end of a long track in a fairly remote part of the country—there is a strong sense that he now attempts to ration visitors. His work has been hugely influential in the country, even more so than Piet's, believes Fleur. "His style is easier for people to understand and do themselves, and he has always done the same sort of thing. Piet's style has changed over the years, and some people found that difficult to follow ... a Piet Oudolf garden appears to look easy to make, but it is difficult to do." Piet and ter Linden's work, however, shares basic characteristics that have also been at the core of the Dutch Wave: the emphasis on a rich selection of perennials and a desire to enter into a dialogue with nature.

Combing the Nurseries

It was natural for Dutch gardeners to turn to Great Britain—and specifically England—for interesting plants, particularly perennials during the 1970s and early 1980s. Germany had some very good large perennial nurseries but, with exceptions, they lacked the vitality and curiosity found in the British small nursery sector. The milder climate of the British Isles was probably a factor too; certain species were capable of thriving there and in The Netherlands but were less likely to survive in Germany's colder winters. In addition, there is no doubting that many Dutch people felt more at home in Britain.

Britain's amazingly vibrant small nursery sector took off during this period, although it had in fact been in existence for some time previously. Prior to the 1960s, perennials were almost unknown in commercial landscape planting and garden perennials were largely selected and marketed on the basis of their contribution to color-based

A planting design by Ton ter Linden.

KARL FOERSTER

Karl Foerster (1874–1970) may possibly go down in history as the most influential gardener ever. A nurseryman and plant breeder, Foerster was also something of a philosopher; this aspect of his approach makes his writing difficult to translate or appreciate for non-German readers. His brother, Friedrich Wilhelm Foerster, was a noted pacifist and one of the most prominent intellectual critics of the Nazi regime. He fled to the U.S. during the war. Foerster was also something of a resistance figure and he sheltered Jewish friends by employing them in the nursery—unlike in Britain, in Germany ornamental plant growing was not immediately banned during the war. Another beneficiary of Foerster's bravery was Walther Funcke, for whom the *Achillea* cultivar is named. A member of the Communist Party, Funcke was jailed for four years by the Nazi regime, then went on to become one of the leading landscape designers of the post-war communist East German state; Foerster provided him with work and cover. Foerster's trademark beret was the mid-twentieth-century headgear of choice for artistic and political radicals; some of his followers, such as Ernst Pagels and Hans Simon, also wore it.

When Foerster took over his parents' nursery in 1903, his mission was to grow a selection of plants from the contemporary "chaos" of cultivars, and to combine beauty with reliability. A few years later he started his famous garden at Bornim in Potsdam, just outside Berlin. Its plan was centered around an English-inspired sunken garden, and it incorporated a variety of habitats that reflected his interest not just in then-fashionable color-themed gardening but in plants of quieter beauty such as ferns and grasses. As a breeder he worked primarily on the very commercial delphiniums, phlox, chrysanthemum, and asters—but also on grasses. In total he bred around 370 varieties.

Foerster became an increasingly prominent writer and radio broadcaster on gardening, and his house and garden became the meeting hub of what was later called the *Bornimer Kreis*—the Bornim circle of garden and landscape designers, but also of architects, writers, artists, and musicians. Gardening in pre–World War II Germany was an activity taken seriously by the cultural elite, and bridged those interested in and appreciative of painting, philosophy, music, and nature. Although the most prominent writer on naturalistic garden design of the period, Willy Lange, had written a foreword to a book of Foerster's, he kept Lange and his natives-only "Nordic garden" at a distance and denounced the Nazi policy of favoring only native German species. He would remind his readers that garden plants, like the food on their tables, "came from the five continents of the earth."

Karl Foerster in 1967.

After the war, Foerster found himself in the Soviet-ruled (i.e. effectively Russian) part of Germany. Honored by the communist regime, he continued to be involved in running the nursery although it had effectively become a state-run enterprise. Indeed, it was the only perennial nursery in the whole country. In retirement he continued to write and was published in both east and west. He was also involved in the design, planting, and restoration of several public gardens, including Goethe's garden in Weimar. His Freundschaftsinsel public garden in Potsdam is today one of the most notable and well-labeled collections of perennials in Germany, and a true survivor—it was commissioned during the Nazi regime, maintained by the communist one, and restored after reunification.

Foerster's legacy consists of many new plant cultivars, a vast body of books and lectures, students who went on to become influential in their own right, and indeed a whole generation of gardeners. Richard Hansen, the founder of "habitat planting," was a pupil, and Wolfgang Oehme of Washington DC's Oehme van Sweden Landscape Architecture, although not taught by him, can be claimed as a "grand-student."

and quite labor-intensive planting schemes. Reading through catalogs of the time, what comes across is the limited range of genera, but the enormous variety—particularly of color variations—in each genera. There was a tendency to specialize: delphinium, aster, chrysanthemum etc. Commercial nurseries in Germany of the period offered a similar selection. However, writers like Margery Fish (1892–1969) and Vita Sackville-West (1892–1962) did much to broaden the horizons of midcentury British gardeners, primarily through regular weekend columns in widely read newspapers, and secondly through books.

The "gray decade" of the 1950s was enlivened for many British women by the rapid growth of flower-arranging clubs inspired, like the gardeners, by practitioner-writers such as Constance Spry (1886–1960). The contemporary flower-arranging style had enormously widened the range of flowers—and foliage and other plant parts—that were considered acceptable. Among the keen amateur florists was Beth Chatto, who took up growing some of the more "unusual" flowers for cutting. So began one of the most influential of all gardening careers. She began with a nursery that opened for business in 1967, and went on to write and lecture extensively. It is hard to overestimate her impact. Possessed of both charm and single-mindedness, Beth proved unstoppable as nurserywoman, exhibitor, and writer. Her early exhibits at the Chelsea Flower Show (the first was in 1976) were criticized by the judges for including plants not then regarded as garden plants, such as astrantias and euphorbias. Another key innovator was Alan Bloom (1906–2005), whose Bressingham Gardens, founded as a nursery and display garden in 1955, also promoted perennials both as plants and features in a new informal planting style. Bloom was one of the key figures behind the Hardy Plant Society, founded in 1957, which enabled a growing number of amateur perennial enthusiasts to keep in touch.

By the early 1980s a considerable network of small nurseries had begun to grow perennials, and enough of a market of keen home gardeners had formed to support them. England, then, was a natural place for Piet to come looking for plants. Fortunately for him, and for many other Dutch gardeners and growers, there was a particular concentration of these nurseries in the affluent southeast corner of England. One only had to

Piet digging out perennials at Alan Bloom's, top,
and Beth Chatto with Mien Ruys, below.

drive over on one of the frequent cross-channel ferries to find something of a horticultural paradise. A key development was the gradual relaxation on phytosanitary controls on taking plants from one country to another—one of the many benefits of British membership in the European Union. The final dropping of any controls on ornamental plants was part of the Schengen Agreement, passed in 1995, which eliminated passport and other controls between many European countries.

Although the German perennial nurseries were not perhaps as innovative as the British, they had a long history of intensive breeding of many perennial genera. Their lists were often very impressive, with more varieties carried over from past breeding than the British, who dropped many cultivars from the 1950s onward. Peter zur Linden and Hagemann were famous for the range of phlox, rodgersia, helenium, astilbe, grass, and fern varieties that they grew, while the great nursery of von Zeppelin, set up by Helen von Stein Zeppelin—the Countess von Zeppelin—in the 1930s was famous for poppies and irises. Plantsman Hans Simon, with a nursery in the Franconia region of Bavaria, recalled that of some of the more chaotic small British nurseries had huge collections natural species, as opposed to hybrids and cultivars.

During this time, Piet travelled several times a year across the German border to the town of Leer to see Ernst Pagels, one of the most distinguished of Germany's nurserymen. Now in his seventies, Pagels, who had been a pupil of Karl Foerster, was still actively running his business and making plant selections. "We went to get the newest plants and to bring them home ... and we exchanged a lot," recalls Piet. Pagels was the source of many plants that went on to become mainstays of Piet's design work, including: *Achillea* 'Walther Funcke,' *Astilbe chinensis* var. *taquetii* 'Purpurlanze,' *Phlomis tuberosa* 'Amazone,' a number of *Salvia nemorosa* cultivars such as 'Amethyst,' 'Blauhügel,' 'Ostfriesland,' 'Rügen,' 'Tänzerin,' and 'Wesuwe,' and *Veronicastrum virginicum* 'Lavendelturm' and 'Diana.'

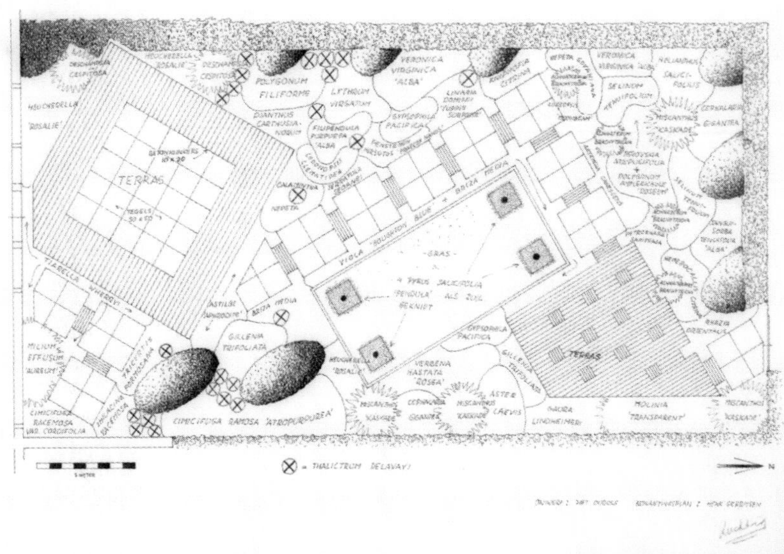

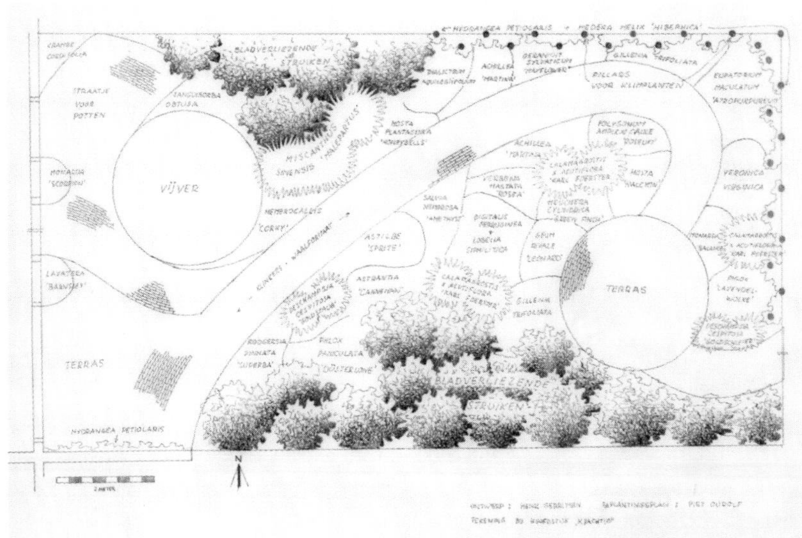

Plans by Oudolf and Henk Gerritsen used in the book *Planting the Natural Garden*.

ERNST PAGELS

Ernst Pagels (1913–2007) was one of the great nurserymen and plant breeders of late-twentieth-century Germany. He had been a frequent visitor to Karl Foerster at his home near Potsdam as a young man and apprentice gardener; inevitably Foerster had become something of a guru figure to Pagels's generation. After the war and a spell as a prisoner of war, he returned home in 1949. He recalled, "it was the first time I had seen Karl Foerster after a nightmarish time. His words, his comfort, his goodness were a balm against deep depression."[3] Among the older man's passing gifts was a packet of seed of *Salvia nemorosa*, a plant common to dry meadows in eastern Germany. That packet started Pagels off on a lifetime of plant selection. From it he selected 'Ostfriesland,' a stunningly good plant with deep blue-purple flowers, a compact habit and, after a prune, a habit of repeat flowering. During his life, Pagels selected 130 perennial cultivars from thirty genera, including thirteen *Salvia*.

His criteria for selecting a cultivar were to do with what we would call "garden-worthiness" as much as instant impact: longevity, a long season of not just flowering but general all-round tidiness, and a relatively compact habit. These traits have led to at least half of his selections still being in commercial production today.

Pagels enjoyed huge respect among colleagues in Germany and The Netherlands, and was among the few German growers who got to be known beyond the borders of these two countries. A visit to his nursery in Leer almost took on the feeling of a pilgrimage—I have felt it myself. I remember Pagels as a physically impressive man who wore a signature beret, who grew the biggest clumps of miscanthus I have ever seen, and for the morel mushrooms popping up in the bark of some of his standing-out beds. I also remember some colorful African shirts—Leer is near Bremen, a major port, and over the years Pagels had befriended several sailors from Ghana. One Ghanaian man in particular, Issa Osman, was very close to Pagels; he became his caretaker in later years and is still very involved in the management of the public garden project that has succeeded the nursery. And of course there was the Ostfriesland tea ceremony—a tradition dating back over two centuries. It consists of strong tea with special sugar crystals and creamy milk, now sold in little cartons as "tea milk."

Slovenian television producer Stane Sušnik also visited Ernst Pagels, and recalls that "I felt very proud that I was able to meet at least some of the people who were so influential in this style of gardening. It helped me realize that all the things we have in our meadows and wood edges could be used, not in the way that they are

Ernst Pagels in 1993.

in nature, but we could pick out species and varieties and join them in large groups and intermingle them."

Garden writer Michael King told me that "We used to have a lunch for his birthday, every year. A lot of Dutch nurserymen would get together ... so many Dutch nursery people regarded him as an important inspiration ... Piet and Anja would always be there, and Hans Kramer, Coen Jansen, Brian Kabbes, Henk Gerritsen came a few times ... we would take him to a nice restaurant, we would buy the lunch, Ernst would sit at the head of the table." When Pagels died, he left the nursery to a foundation that now runs it as a Rudolf Steiner kindergarten and public park featuring an extensive collection of the plants he raised.

Henk Gerritsen's and Anton Schlepers' influential Priona garden.

Meeting a Kindred Spirit

Piet and Anja had initially set up their nursery to grow plants to supply Piet's garden design business, but the nursery, as we now know, took off with a life of its own. Garden enthusiasts came to buy his plants, especially unusual and new ones. The nursery helped the Oudolfs become known, earn some money, and meet new people. One of the earliest visitors was Henk Gerritsen.

Henk wielded considerable influence as a gardener among the wider public: those who made the pilgrimage to the Mien Ruys Garden at Dedemsvaart could see his Priona in the same trip. Gerritsen continued to write until his death, and he also made an impact as a consultant, most notably at Waltham Place in Berkshire, England. This early-twentieth-century formal garden is now home to one of the most self-consciously wild-style gardens in the country, thanks to owner Strilli Oppenheimer, who employed Henk to guide her and her staff—headed by Beatrice Krehl, who had previously been head gardener at the Mien Ruys Garden.

Piet's visits to Priona and discussions with Henk were very important in his development as a designer. "Henk was guiding the planting into a natural setting," Piet recalls. "When we started to talk, I was trying to develop planting design and not really getting it. I found what I was doing was not spontaneous enough." By looking at Priona, Piet began to loosen up his design style. "With Henk," Piet says, "I learned that planting is also to do with plant structure, shape and caracter. Ambience, seasonality, emotion—these are important. With Henk, we discovered plants that were good even when they were not flowering. He pointed this out to me a hundred times. We looked at plants at times other than their prime time." Henk and Piet helped each other to develop what has become a fundamentally new way of designing and planting.

HENK GERRITSEN

Henk Gerritsen (1948–2008) first arrived at Hummelo in 1982 as a customer. "He had seen our small catalog," Piet recalled. "He said he had never seen a catalog like it before, he bought some plants, he came back, and we started to talk." Henk remembers the nursery "as a revelation. I just kept going back ... his plants were different, plants nobody knew ... he had an assortment in subtle shades and that looked wilder than others. [He paid] attention to the appearance of the plants after flowering: seed heads, autumn colors, winter silhouettes." Later, Piet and Anja and the boys went to visit the garden Henk was making with Anton Schlepers. Piet remembers experiencing the Priona garden as "completely wild—wildflowers were integrated with nursery plants." Above all, he understood and liked Henk's credo of "playing with nature."

Priona began as a joint project between Henk and Anton, a photographer. Anton had been the artistic part of the garden partnership, Henk the naturalist and ecologist. Anton died in 1993, after which Henk continued alone. The garden became a vital part of his memory of Anton. Both had been deeply inspired by the wildflower communities of Europe and, guided by Henk's considerable knowledge of ecology, they tried to bring as much of the feeling of wild meadows and other plant communities into the garden as possible. The garden was deliberately unkempt, but included areas of mown grass, hedges, and other aspects of the more conventional garden. A variety of sculptures and topiaries helped to create an eccentric—indeed humorous—atmosphere. By the standards of some naturalistic gardens developed in the 1990s it would not have rated as very wild, but when the two men began to open the garden to the public in the early 1980s, it was clear from the reactions of some visitors that what they were doing was unconventional. It was not universally understood or appreciated.

Like many of the city dwellers who moved to the country, Henk and Anton infused their rural life with a strong romantic streak. When they attempted to grow vegetables for the first time, they were overwhelmed with pests and bolting plants, and interpreted this to mean that they were not cut out to be farmers. Seeing the vegetable flowers and seed heads as having a certain distinct beauty of their own, however, they then started to grow vegetables deliberately to let them go to seed. They enjoyed seeing the tall, gangly stems of leek, cabbage, and parnsip flowers alongside annuals and wildflowers. For some visitors, this part of the garden was almost shocking.

Priona, and Henk's work in general, was promoted by Elisabeth de Lestrieux, an interior designer and writer of garden and cookbooks. She was friendly with Rob Leopold and others in the gardening world, and Henk named one of the last

From left to right: Henk Gerritsen, Anja Oudolf, Eric Brown (Rosie Atkins's husband), a botanist, Piet Oudolf, and Metka Zigon, on a tour looking at wildflowers in Slovenia in 2000.

parts of the garden he developed after her nickname, Kaatje. Kaatje's Garden features a central mass of yew clipped into abstract organic forms that are vaguely reminiscent of abstract sculpture. This is surrounded by ornamental grasses and wildflowers. As a modernist expression of the creative tension between wildness and topiary, it makes a big impact on visitors.

For many gardeners, Priona became known through Marijke Heuff's photography. She captured a particular quality of the garden that has since become very influential: rank masses of seed heads, dead stems, and fading foliage. Marijke marinated the chaos and decay in warm autumn sunlight, and began to persuade many people of the value of seed heads as a result. For Henk, who was struggling with the death of his partner from AIDS and his own ill health, this particular aspect of the garden became an important one, but not in a lugubrious or macabre way. "People used to be so afraid of death in the garden," Henk said to me once. "Every yellow leaf was an imperfection, and had to be taken out ... but now a whole generation has known death, so we do not ban it from the garden anymore." By the 2000s, however, he felt he had made his point, and said that he did not want Priona to be known as "the death garden" anymore. After he died in 2008, a period of uncertainty regarding the garden's future led a group of friends to take on its upkeep. Although it has since been sold, the new owners are sympathetic to his ideals, and it is open to the public once again.

When publisher Terra asked Piet to write a book in 1989, he realized that writing was not his forté; he turned to Henk for help. Together they discussed their favorite plants, Henk wrote the text, and Anton did the photography. Their idea was that their names would take equal billing on the cover; the publisher had other ideas, wanting only Piet's name, a recognition perhaps of his growing fame at the time. Piet had to insist on Henk's name getting its rightful place. During that year's very hot summer Anton labored in the garden and at Hummelo, sometimes in temperatures above 86°F (30°C); Henk wrote the text over the next winter, sitting in front of an electric fire. The publication the year after of *Droomplanten* (*Dreamplants*) launched a distinct perennial selection into the world. A Swedish edition followed remarkably quickly and, nine years later, a subsequent volume, *Méér Droomplanten* (*More Dreamplants*). The latter was published in English in 1999 as *Dreamplants for the Natural Garden*, and the original *Droomplanten* appeared as *Planting the Natural Garden* in 2003. In 1993, the year of Anton's death, he and Henk published a book of their own, *Spelen met de natuur* (*Playing with Nature*), about their experiences traveling to look at wildflowers and their attempts at bringing their discoveries into the garden.

It is interesting and still instructive to read through *Planting the Natural Garden.* The chapter headings say a lot about the concepts Piet and Henk were discussing at the time. They categorize plants in a design-led way, which conventional plant-reference books almost never did. The titles are also quirky: Blazing, Lush, Airy, Tranquillity, Exuberant, Silvery, Grassy, Gloomy?, Autumn, Wonderful. Another chapter, headed 'Good Neighbors,' highlights the importance of thinking about perennials in combination. Speaking as a professional writer, I must say that I love Henk's writing style. It's laid back, laconic, richly informative, witty, and honest—he is the garden writer whose work I admire and seek to emulate the most.

FLORA
KWEKERIJ
OUDOLF

Henk Gerritsen, Anja Oudolf, and Piet Oudolf, top.
An open day at Hummelo, below.

Open Days: A New Way of Meeting

The plant fair is so much a part of contemporary garden life that it is hard to remember the time when there was no such thing as nursery owners turning up in vans, setting out plants, and waiting anxiously as customers descend. The first hour or so is generally a mad rush of plant connoisseurs scanning the stalls for rarities or plants on their want lists. Once it settles down to a more sedate pace, discussions turn to earnest conversations between customer and vendor, or less-earnest ones where the stall holders patiently explain some point they themselves find very elementary.

During the 1980s there was a marked growth of interest across Northern Europe in gardening and garden history. In Britain, some of the best plant fairs were organized by county groups of the newly formed National Council for the Conservation of Plants and Gardens.[4] I myself had a small nursery at the time, and can vividly recall selling at many fairs. In some cases, the search for rare plants could get quite heated: I remember that when the deep scarlet *Knautia macedonica* first appeared, respectable English county ladies were almost fighting over it. Now it can be found in virtually any garden center.

The establishment of so many plant fairs over a short period of time is one of those examples of the zeitgeist at work. A few get started independently of each other, then a lot of other people emulate the idea. In September 1983 there was a plant fair at Hortus Haren, near Groningen, while in October, a plant fair with a dozen nurseries was held at the Domaine de Courson, south of Paris. The latter is today the premier event of its kind in Europe. The same year, on the last weekend in August, the Oudolfs held their first Open Day at Hummelo.

"Our idea was to bring people together," says Piet. "Of course we wanted to create some income, but thought it would also be a good idea to bring a selection of growers who share the same interest in plants, as an advertisement for all of us." The Oudolfs sold their own plants, and other nurseries and plant-related businesses were invited to sell their wares too. "We didn't have many other nurseries join us the very first year, but we had Rob [Leopold] with his seeds, Rita van der Zalm and her bulbs, and Ploeger, a nursery run by brothers Wout and Dick Ploeger. Because of Romke, Christopher Lloyd came along for a visit too." In subsequent years, more nurseries were invited, including Coen Jansen and de Kleine Plantage. In 1987, some other traders came too, including Elisabeth de Lestrieux, two antiquarian booksellers, and people who sold specialty tools. Anja did much of the organizing and arranged the publicity.

After the first year, the event was always held on the first weekend in September. Initially visitors numbered in the hundreds, but that quickly built up to thousands. In the beginning, they were just from Holland and Belgium, but later people would come from Denmark, Sweden, and Germany. There were no parking facilities, so cars just had to park along the road. Coen Jansen was an early participant, and remembers that "we were all young nurserymen showing and selling our plants ... Piet didn't charge anything whatsoever ... He has always been very clever and he has a very good talent for advertising ... but he's not egotistical. We were all there on equal terms." For a young generation of gardeners and nurserymen, the Open Days were also an opportunity to get ideas and plants, meet people, make contacts, and introduce themselves. The garden world is an extraordinarily open and friendly one. Practitioners readily pass on seeds, cuttings, addresses, and telephone numbers.

By 1997, however, the Open Days had run their course. With so many other events popping up all over the country the original no longer seemed special, so the Oudolfs made the decision to take a weekend later in September and have Grass Days instead, which celebrated one of the key plant groups they were working with and wished to promote. Talks by leading garden personalities such as Roy Lancaster, Jelena de Belder, and Penelope Hobhouse were given to a wide range of invited guests who represented the most forward-looking of Europe's gardeners. "It was a big party," recalls Rosie Atkins, the first editor of *Gardens Illustrated* magazine. "A bit like Courson, with stands. I met some good people, like Sneeboer, who make handmade tools ... what I liked most was Anja and all her girlfriends who used to help. We'd have lots of bowls of pea soup and sit around talking plants."

Looking back, it's clear that the Hummelo Open Days enabled Piet and Anja not only to introduce themselves to the world, but also to meet many other likeminded people and to network. Rosie, for example, remembers that "Piet introduced me to Marijke Heuff at an early Open Day, and she was a huge source of pictures of new gardens we hadn't seen

in the U.K." In particular, Piet remembers meeting Rob Leopold on their first Open Day weekend. "We had heard about him and Cruydt-Hoeck from Henk Gerritsen. So I phoned Rob. He was interested and wanted to join us right away. In the tunnel greenhouse that was to the rear of our house, Rob hung all his seed packets for display. I thought it wonderful. I had never seen anything like it." Piet even partly attributes the continuing success of the Open Days to Rob: "He gave us both practical support … for example by helping Anja with the organization of the publicity for the nursery. He did that sort of thing for so many people, and he was always connecting people with one another with tremendous energy."

The Open Days became far more than simply an opportunity to sell and promote businesses—they became a social and intellectual exchange too. "Rob always wanted me to explain what it was that motivated me in my work, where it all came from," says Piet. "This ongoing discussion was sort of a repeating circle, going one stage deeper every time—or one should probably say higher, until it touched heaven. Rob became a very dear friend, and our conversations after the Open Days always continued until two or three o'clock in the morning. They were always about the depth, the width, the plenitude of things."

Ewald Hügin was one of the first to attend the Open Days from Germany. He was then a young man just starting out—today his nursery in the middle of the city of Freiburg in Germany's Black Forest region is one of the most exciting plantsman nurseries in Europe. It bursts with both novel hardy perennials and tender species for summer planting. Coen Jansen also remembers a younger man who came to the Open Days, but as a customer, not as a seller: Hans Kramer. Hans went on to become one of the great innovators on the Dutch nursery scene, both in terms of his plant range and his work on potting composts.

The Hummelo Open Days in fact have had a local successor. In 1996, the first Nursery Day was held at Huis Bingerden, practically down the road from the Oudolfs, toward Arnhem. Eugénie van Weede had been to the first Courson event, and her husband had thought it would be marvellous to have something similar at Bingerden. A few years later she asked Piet, Rob, and Romke to lunch. "They were all very enthusiastic," she recalls. "They helped us choose the initial nursery vendors. We think of them as the three founders, or 'godfathers' in Dutch." Starting with thirty stalls,

Jelena de Belder with Penelope Hobhouse, top,
and Rob Leopold, below.

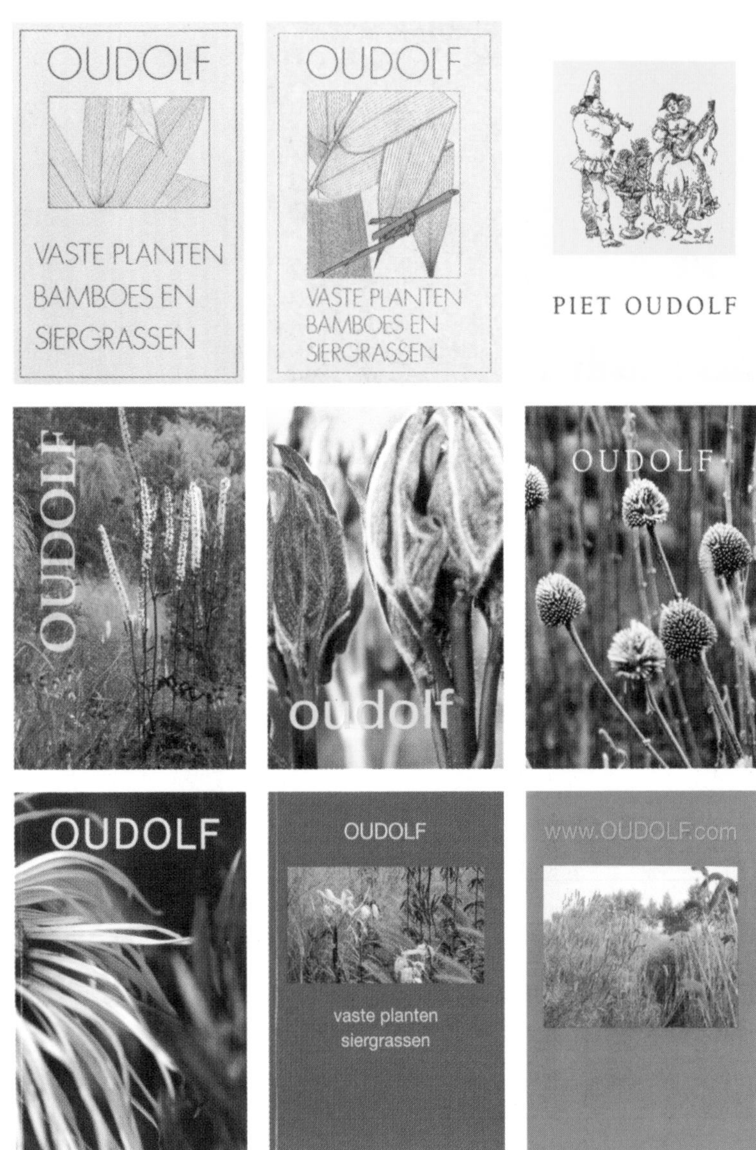

Historical catalog covers from the Oudolf nursery.

the number has today grown to over a hundred, and the event has indeed become the "Dutch Courson." Eugénie affirms that the intent is still pure, however. "[We only sell] plants and things to do with plants. We don't have napkins and scented candles."

By the late 1980s, the first phase of Piet's "research and development" era was over. With a plant range he felt confident in, a circle of likeminded people around him, and the first shoots of a definite boom in gardening across northwest Europe, it was a good place to be. But there was a long way to go before either Piet or the new look perennial garden were established.

Anja Oudolf in the trial garden.

Anja's favorites

Achillea 'Walther Funcke'
Aconitum 'Stainless Steel'
Actaea pachypoda
A. 'Scimitar'
Adelocaryum anchusoides
Allium 'Summer Beauty'
Amsonia tabernaemontana var. *salicifolia*
Anemone rivularis
Aralia californica
Asclepias incarnata
A. tuberosa
Aster 'Little Carlow'
A. 'Alma Pötschke'
A. oblongifolius 'October Skies'
Astrantia 'Roma'
A. major subsp. *involucrata* 'Shaggy'

Baptisia leucantha
Brunnera macrophylla 'Jack Frost'

Centranthus ruber
C. r. var. *coccineus*
Ceratostigma plumbaginoides
Chamerion (epilobium) angustifolium 'Album'
Chrysanthemum 'Paul Boissier'
Clematis heracleifolia 'China Purple'
C. recta 'Purpurea'

Deinanthe bifida
Darmera peltata

Echinacea purpurea 'Vintage Wine'
Eupatorium maculatum 'Riesenschirm'

Foeniculum vulgare 'Giant Bronze'

Geranium wallichianum 'Buxton's Variety'
Geum 'Flames of Passion'
Gillenia trifoliata
Glycyrrhiza yunnanensis

Helenium 'Die Blonde'
Hosta plantaginea var. *grandiflora*

Liatris borealis

Pycnanthemum muticum

Salvia × sylvestris 'Dear Anja'
Sanguisorba canadensis
Selinum wallichianum
Serratula seoanei

Thalictrum delavayi 'Album'
T. 'Elin'

Vernonia crinita 'Mammuth'
Veronicastrum virginicum 'Adoration'
V. v. 'Temptation'

Grasses and sedges

Carex bromoides
Chrysopogon gryllus

Eragrostis spectabilis

Miscanthus sinensis 'Gewitterwolke'
M. s. 'Samurai'
Molinia caerulea subsp. *caerulea* 'Moorhexe'

Panicum virgatum 'Shenandoah'

Sorghastrum nutans
Spodiopogon sibiricus
Sporobolus heterolepis
Stipa tirsa

BECOMING KNOWN

By the late 1980s, Piet Oudolf was attracting new clients—and the nursery a growing circle of customers. Members of Britain's Hardy Plant Society were among the first from outside the country to "discover" him and Anja. A member of the society wrote a report of a trip to visit Hummelo in its newsletter in 1987; it starts off by reinforcing that the Dutch were known traditionally as bulb producers and not as growers of perennials, but she noted that "the Dutch knowledge of, and interest in, hardy plants is extraordinary and is growing fast and I believe that they have a great future in this field." On their second day the visitors "started an hour's journey to Hummelo, near Arnhem, where Piet Oudolf, a landscape designer, runs his 1.3 acre nursery and garden. Both reflect his design ability combined with a flair for color. For his landscape work he grows the best of each variety, chosen for hardiness. *Cimicifuga atropurpurea* was very much in evidence, with pretty *Aster* 'Sonora,' *Achnatherum brachytricha*, a two-and-a-half-foot-tall grass with an intriguing cone-shaped head. My eyes were riveted by the beauty of *Miscanthus* 'Malepartus' ... all the grasses here grow well and have much larger flower heads than most in cultivation. Amongst his superb collection ... the most outstanding was *M.* 'Rotfuchs,' tall and strong to 6ft with close, thick flowerheads, an obvious choice for landscaping. Not being too familiar with the genus *Miscanthus*, I was overwhelmed by them all, many being new varieties from Germany ... the grasses and bamboos were outstanding and left a deep impression on me."[1]

Two private gardens Oudolf designed in the late 1980s, the van Steeg garden, top, and the Pattenotte/van der Laan garden, below.

One early client was Hans van Steeg. Working on a part of the garden that was approximately 13,000 square feet (1,200 square meters), Piet had ample scope to create something befitting the scale of his signature perennials and grasses. His large borders of big perennials were surrounded by agricultural land, making them seem like a parallel, ornamental version of the muscular maize crops that often surrounded the property in summer. Near the house was an inward-looking and private garden of clipped yew and box. At last, Piet had created a showpiece garden, and in particular an opportunity for him to photograph his work at all times of year and in all weather. Mr. van Steeg had a clothing factory in Croatia that he visited annually; one year he invited Piet to join him on the trip, giving him the opportunity to visit a country in a region whose rich biodiversity has contributed so much to our gardens.

With the house now renovated and a garden that he could feel proud of, Piet felt Hummelo was ready to show to potential clients. On one of my first visits, Piet said to me that "if anyone contacts me and wants to talk to me about designing a garden, I tell them to come here and look first." The early 1990s saw him working on a number of private garden commissions and some commercial projects—developers suddenly wanted plantings around new office blocks that had a bit more character than the usual sprawl of evergreen shrubs. One such project, in 1991, was for the printer Van Elburg at Sassenheim. Piet laid out over 21,000 square feet (2,000 square meters) of borders for the company.

Opportunities also arose that allowed Piet to make excursions beyond the Dutch border to look at, buy, or collect plants. On November 9, 1989 the Berlin Wall, which had so cruelly divided the people of Germany, between a NATO member (the Federal Republic) and a Russian puppet state, the DDR (German Democratic Republic), was officially opened by a reformist leadership in the DDR. A week later, as crowds of East Germans were swarming over the border to stare at the variety of consumer goods available in the shop windows of West Germany, Piet and Coen Jansen drove east. Their destination was the garden and nursery of Karl Foerster at Bornim, a suburb of Potsdam near Berlin.

Foerster had died in 1970 at the age of ninety-six, but his wife, Eva, and daughter, Marianne, were still living in the house. Its famous sunken garden had now become much overshadowed by trees. Piet remembers that there was "nowhere to stay, as everyone was wanting to be in Berlin to look around and do business ... we ended up staying in the nursery sheds." The nursery still existed, but he recalls that "it was a state-owned enterprise ... everything was grown in an agricultural way, in the ground, in fields." As always under communism, the manager had developed other ways of boosting his income—Piet and Coen discovered that "he had his own patch where he grew plants that he sold himself at weekend markets." Among them, Piet says, "I remember that we found *Salvia nemorosa* 'Plumosa' in the back garden. Coen bought some delphiniums, but there was little of real value left, no hidden rarities to discover."

Led to Hummelo by word of mouth, the occasional magazine article, and, for many, the attraction of potentially discovering new plants in the nursery, the number of visitors began to grow. The first indications that Piet's reputation was beginning to seep beyond the Dutch border were apparent. In 1991 Piet was invited to be a judge at the Journées des Plantes at Courson. There, on an old estate south of Paris, with a beautiful park laid out in the "English manner" of informal arrangements of trees and water, Patrice and Hélène Fustier and Olivier and Patricia de Nervaux-Loys have run a twice-yearly plant fair since 1983. Nurseries from all over France—and some from Belgium, The Netherlands, and Britain—come to sell plants to an enthusiastic public. Nursery stands and plants are also judged by a jury of distinguished garden professionals. In 1991, having been invited to join the jury, Piet remained a member for ten years. His colleagues on the panel were Roy Lancaster, the most renowned of Great Britain's plantsmen, and Hans Simon, a German nurseryman who had long championed the use of perennials.

Courson was where Lancaster introduced Piet to Rosie Atkins in the early nineties. Rosie at the time was editor, indeed the founding editor, of the London-based magazine *Gardens Illustrated.* Crucially, she was the first person to write about Piet in an English-language publication. An article about him and Hummelo appeared in the seventh issue of the magazine, in April 1994. Since then, almost every one of his gardens and landscape projects of importance have been featured by the magazine as well.

Rosie and her husband, Eric, went on to become very good friends with Piet and Anja. "It was love at first sight," says Rosie. "We definitely

Oudolf's arrival in East Germany soon after the wall fell, top, and Anja Oudolf with Rosie Atkins, founding editor of the U.K.'s *Gardens Illustrated* magazine, below.

Collecting I

Piet and Anja have always collected studio pottery. I certainly remember a time when the quantity of ceramics threatened to overwhelm the kitchen. In recent years, Anja has focused her collecting efforts on the ceramics of the Bloomsbury group, and Quentin Bell's in particular.

Britain's artistic and intellectual Bloomsbury group has long been a source of popular fascination. Active in the 1920s, they brought bright colors, naive charm, liberal thinking, and creative insights to art and literature. Some of the group lived, semi-collectively, at an old farmhouse in Sussex, called Charleston. The property is open to the public and acts as an unofficial museum for the group. Quentin Bell (1910–1996) was the son of Clive and Vanessa Bell and the nephew of Virginia Woolf. He was the only member of the group to truly explore ceramics, although he was better known as a writer, most notably as the author of the definitive biography of his famous aunt. He trained in the great pottery town of Stoke-on-Trent as a young man and went on to make pottery all his life. He played a crucial role in the preservation of Charleston in the 1960s. His pottery is known for its naive quality and its colors, which are the result of Bell's mixing his own glazes and his trials with firing temperatures.

Anja recalls how she "first got interested in the pottery when we went to Charleston in the mid-eighties, when Piet was visiting nurseries in the area. I fell in love with it, the look of everything ... We found the gallery in London where you can buy sketches and paintings by the group, the Bloomsbury Workshop, but it was Quentin Bell's ceramics I fell for. I love the combination of colors. We buy a few pieces every year." Charleston has now become a regular stop on trips over to England. Through the gallery, Piet and Anja have even arranged to visit Olive, Bell's widow, who is now in her nineties.

had chemistry. At that stage he didn't speak very good English, but the four of us got on together so very well ... There are parallels: we were both brought up in the hospitality business (my parents had a hotel business), we both had two children, we like the same clothes, art, and jazz and blues. Eric and Anja and Piet love opera ... Anja and I love rootling around charity shops. Anja collects Bloomsbury ceramics—I've helped her with that ... and we are all very interested in architecture. The only mismatch is that they don't cook."

Rosie recalls that "the first thing I wrote about Piet was that he was like an artist grinding his own colors when he grows the plants himself, and sometimes collects and breeds them. The whole process is his, he created his own palette and used that palette in an appropriate way for the site ... his almost obsessive drawings, all hand done, have an artist's quality. I went to art school and a lot of my friends are painters; he reminds me so much of a painter, as opposed to other landscape designers I know. He's so much more intense and not always so sure of how to express himself." Rosie also notes that "Anja's role in keeping everything calm and making sure everything runs smoothly allows him to work. It's like she is an artist's muse."

Gardens Illustrated magazine played a crucial role in promoting good garden design—and continues to do so. While not entirely focused on contemporary design, let alone associated with any particular school or movement, it reflects the *now*, specifically what garden-makers of all kinds, from landscape architects to amateurs, are doing to invent and reinvent ways of making the garden a crucial breathing space for humanity. Perhaps because gardens and garden-making are a psychological survival mechanism for so many people, there is a strong tendency toward the romantic. In turn, nostalgia for the past manifests itself easily as backward-looking design. This is something the magazine has never indulged, and sets it apart from its competitors.

Gardens Illustrated magazine was launched in 1992, but started life the year before as a pilot project for a publisher that wisely involved Rosie Atkins, formerly an editor with *The Sunday Times Magazine.* When the economics did not work out, she took the dummy issues to John Brown Publishing, which took it on. The basic idea was that it would sell on the strength of the images. "It was me starting it," says Rosie, "on my own. The wife of the publisher worked as art editor, but she hadn't done any graphics at all really ... I set it up by taking people out to lunch at River Café, asking them to take pictures, telling them I couldn't afford to pay them, and saying I didn't want pictures from their library that we would have all seen before in the other magazines—they had to be fresh images." Garden photography as a profession was in its infancy at the time, with very few practitioners. "People like Andrew Lawson were just amazing to me, giving me free pictures," Atkins said. "We blagged some trips for them, paid them in River Café lunches. It worked because it was an international magazine, but it had some lifestyle in it, it assumed readers were interested in what the owners wore, what they ate."

"Piet introduced me to so many people," Rosie told me. "James van Sweden and Wolfgang Oehme, for example. Much of what went into the magazine was built on these relationships in the early days ... I was trying to make it forward-looking and distinctive since we were getting distributed abroad too."

International Contacts

As the Oudolfs' reputation grew, so did their count of international contacts and friendships. Canadians Nori and Sandra Pope, for example, were a couple the Oudolfs met at a conference at Alnarp, Sweden, in 1992 and kept in touch with for many years. The Popes were gardening at Hadspen House in Somerset, where between 1988 and 2005 they created one of the most talked-about gardens in Britain, and one of the most passionately loved. Although the Popes' style was very different from Piet's—it focused on color above all—he admired their work. A series of color-themed borders and a program of rigorous experimentation allowed them to create one of the most sophisticated color-based gardens ever seen.

Another pair of immensely creative landscape architects the Oudolfs have come to know were James van Sweden and Wolfgang Oehme. Oehme was a horticulturalist who had been trained in Germany in the Foerster tradition—in the DDR, in fact—before emigrating to the U.S. in 1957. Eventually he teamed up with James van Sweden, an architect of Dutch extraction who had studied in The Netherlands in the 1960s and who had discovered early in his career that he "was more interested

Left to right, top: Nori and Sandra Pope, glassblower Anders Wingørd, and Anja Oudolf. James van Sweden and Oudolf, below.

in the spaces between buildings than the buildings themselves," which led him to become a landscape architect. Together they formed the firm today called Oehme van Sweden Landscape Architecture, based in Washington, D.C. Their practice is particularly noted for introducing perennials into urban landscapes. Wolfgang's obsessive interest in plants led him to species and cultivars that could cope with the rigors of life in public spaces; James's vision guided them to create harmonious but graphically strong landscapes.

"Van Sweden came to Hummelo three times" says Piet. "He loved it, and he liked us because we were not traditional." For James, breaking the mold and finding a new way was fundamental. He did, however, find keeping up with Piet's descriptions of plants a bit difficult—in-depth plant knowledge was not his strength and he never really understood the clipped woody elements so important in Piet's work at this time. Most of the pervasive, clipped shrubs in the U.S. are shaped in such a clichéd way and the plants are of such poor quality that most progressive American landscape architects have a strong gut reaction against any clipped forms at all.

In March 1991, Piet and Hans van Steeg visited Croatia and Bosnia, primarily to find and collect hellebores. It was just two weeks before the conflict between the newly independent Croatia and the Serbian-led forces from Yugoslavia began. Although Yugoslavia—which until 1991 consisted of six semiautonomous republics, all of them rich in plant biodiversity—had been the most open of the Eastern European communist states, relatively few plant hunters had been there. Its breakup seemed to have stimulated a lot of interest, particularly in its hellebores. "It was all a big hellebore race," says Piet of that time. His collection contributed to the gene pool available for cultivation, but he himself did not get involved with breeding them. As an element in early spring interest and as long-season foliage plants, he sees hellebores as very important, especially given their longevity and resilience to occasional drought and to cold.

With the collapse of much of former Yugoslavia into war, further travelling in the area became unpopular, although British plantsman and retired professor of mathematics Will McLewin frequently returned to the area to collect hellebore seeds. His inability to speak any of the local

Hunting for plants in Croatia.

languages was a vital protection, as he saw it, against anyone suspecting him of spying. Piet and Anja visited Croatia again with Henk Gerritsen in 1999 and 2000. Slovenia, the most northerly of the former Yugoslav republics, remained peaceful after a short skirmish, and rapidly became known as something of a botanical paradise. Piet returned in 1999 with Rosie Atkins and Eric. Rosie remembers travelling with Henk, too, on one of the trips: "He was an amazing botanist. Anja and Eric would be laid-back, sometimes would go to a café for awhile. Whereas Piet and I would be scrabbling around in the scrub on slopes, looking for plants."

At some stage in the mid-nineties, Slovenia discovered Piet in return. Stane Sušnik was working on some programs for the Slovene state television company with Jelena de Belder, a compatriot married to Flemish diamond merchant Robert de Belder. Together, the couple had created one of Europe's great collections of trees and shrubs, the Kalmthout Arboretum near Antwerp. Jelena suggested one day that Stane go and visit Piet in Hummelo. "It was a funny story," Stane recalls. "Piet agreed to our visit ... but when we arrived we realized that they were having some sort of important personal celebration, something like a wedding anniversary. They were having a meal at home, it was nothing posh at all, it was all very modest. They were just home, very relaxed, so we fell into their very intimate day ... of course we were still shown around the garden." Stane fell in love with Hummelo, and soon the garden was starring on Slovene television.

Stane and his wife, Mojca, have had a major impact on amateur gardening in their country. They set up and ran the country's first gardening magazine, *Roze & VRT* (*Flowers and Garden*), in 2002 and began to organize tours for readers to events in Germany and to the Chelsea Flower Show, as well as to individual gardens, including of course Hummelo. "They are always amazed," Stane says, "because that is the first time that they will have seen that type of planting within a formal frame, especially the grasses." Stane has hosted Piet, Henk, and others—including myself—on visits to his amazingly varied country, and has taken us to the many different habitats that can be found within a couple of hours' drive from the capital, Ljubljana. Stane particularly remembers Piet collecting *Salvia pratensis* varieties, "everything from white to pink and blue; he was amazed at the range."

Anja Oudolf and Dan Pearson, top.
John Coke and prairie specialist Neil Diboll, below.

Another important contact, made in 1991, was Englishman John Coke. Piet and Anja were visiting England and on their way back from seeing the Popes at Hadspen when they were called in to Jenkyn Place, the home of the Coke family. The estate then had a notable garden created by Gerald and Patricia Coke, John's parents. "The head gardener there told me about a nursery, Green Farm Plants, run by John, and said I should meet him," recalls Piet. "On one of my next travels I dropped in ... we immediately established a connection." John recalls "a tall blond-haired figure striding into the nursery ... I knew at once it must be Piet. We had all heard of him by then. We started to chat, and struck up a good rapport." A year later John visited Hummelo, "I can clearly remember the garden. We take these plants for granted now, but then they seemed so new. My eyes were on stalks." After they made initial contact, Piet recalls how "John came to visit us many times. He was very interested to see how we looked at plants, and was always asking questions about why I do things the way I do. He was interested that we were so influenced by the Germans, because he felt they had a different way of doing things."

Piet and John traveled together several times, including three times to the U.S. John remembers that "we were there in 2001 when the towers came down. We visited Roy Diblik, Rick Darke, North Creek Nurseries, and Chanticleer—which neither he nor I liked really at all. It was too bitty and too pretty, they didn't grow his range of plants, and he failed to see eye-to-eye with the director, Chris Woods." Chris, an Englishman who started his career as a gardener at Portmeirion in North Wales, is undoubtedly a brilliant garden entrepreneur, but is a rather larger-than-life character and his strongly theatrical approach to both people and gardens is not to everyone's liking. On another occasion, John recalls that "Piet wanted to visit a Frank Lloyd Wright house, but got the directions wrong somehow, so we ended up in some sort of awful Disney type of funfair. It was dreadful." Traveling together gave Piet an opportunity to share new experiences of plants, gardens, and landscapes with someone who understood his core ideas.

Promoting a Vision

The year 1992 happened to be a year of the Floriade—a horticultural extravaganza held in The Netherlands once a decade. It is a very commercial event, dominated by the big, mass-production growers that form such an important part of the Dutch economy. As something of a reaction to it, a group of small growers got together to form the Groep Traditionele Kwekers (Traditional Growers Group). "We wanted to show ourselves as different from the other nurseries. We wanted to show how involved we are with what we are growing, that we are not so focused on profit," recalls Brian Kabbes. "It was a marketing opportunity for us—we even had a logo." Brian started young in the nursery business and, as with so many others, he was introduced to Piet by Rob Leopold. He has gone on to be a leading innovator with perennials. Apart from Piet, other members of the group included Coen Jansen, Hans Kramer, Eleanore de Koning, and Herman Van Beusekom. The growers' group had their own area at the Floriade—a garden designed by Piet. He remembers it as "having to be laid out in a circular pattern within the triangular space we had been allocated, so that it would be possible for visitors to look around and see the variety of plants we were growing." The group's exhibit was awarded a gold medal.

During this same period, Piet became involved with a number of other exhibitions put on to promote gardening and garden design as well. Such events were becoming more frequent and popular in other Western European countries at the time, thanks in part to rising incomes and, for some, an increase in available leisure time. Businesses involved in domestic gardening saw a booming profit. In 1994 an exhibition was held at Het Loo, one of The Netherlands's most important historical gardens. It was run by *Residence*, an upmarket lifestyle magazine. Piet remembers the event seeming "like a garden or country fair. They asked me to do some decorative plantings of grasses and perennials in lead-covered wood containers. It was our first solo exhibition. Daniel Ost made flower arrangements in the urns with plants from our garden." Ost is a Belgian florist with an international reputation for adventurous work. Another exhibition garden was the one Piet designed for Modeltuinen, a permanent exhibition site at Nieuw Zeggelaar, in Lunteren, near

Amersfoort. The prolific garden writer and entrepreneur Rob Herwig launched the program in 1973, and it ran until 2000. Garden designers from all over the country were invited to build model gardens.

Gardening and landscape work can be a lonely job, but there is also a strong desire, particularly on the part of the more plant-focused, to travel. Seeing other gardens and wild places where interesting species grow or can be collected and meeting other enthusiasts is a source of continual inspiration. Much of the traveling is intimately associated with seeing colleagues, who are almost without exception very generous with their time. Piet traveled and lectured with Roy Lancaster in the U.S. in 1994, and visited the Olympic Peninsula in Washington state in the Pacific Northwest region. "We met Dan Hinkley and went on a tour organized by him and Gil and Carolyn Schieber and a few others. The Schiebers had a mad plantsman's garden. It was inspiring—a lot of local natives ... the mountains smelled of *Phlox divaricata*, and there was castilleja and lupin too." Dan Hinkley has an international reputation, and in the U.S. is famous for the Heronswood Nursery, which he ran on Bainbridge Island, near Seattle, from 1987 to 2000. He also lectures, writes, and participates in plant collection expeditions to East Asia.

Two years later, Piet went to see Urs Walser, director of the Sichtungsgarten Hermannshof in Weinheim, Germany. This garden is one of the best examples of a *Sichtungsgarten*, a place that functions as ornamental exhibition and gives gardeners space for trials of planting combinations. Both professionals and amateurs can appreciate and study plants and plant groups there. "Weinheim shows what you can do with habitats," explains Piet. "It was a new world, with whole new combinations, and completely different to English gardens. I was interested because it was what I wanted to do—to get away from English gardening—but also to escape the dogmas of Richard Hansen." Urs himself came to Hummelo soon afterward, and was also astonished at the confidence and boldness with which Piet used perennials.

Richard Hansen taught planting design at the Munich Technical High School at Weihenstephan,[2] and was the author of a highly influential textbook on planting, published in 1993 in English as *Perennials and Their Garden Habitats*. The book provided an introduction to the whole

concept of thinking about *communities* of plants, but his work had not addressed aesthetics in a clear way, something Urs Walser recognized while designing Hermannshof, to which he brought a very artistic eye. Hansen's work was also undeniably used as a series of planting formulae by some practitioners, hence Piet's barbed comment about "dogmas." Hansen's approach was a revelation to me, however; I remember the exact moment in 1994 when it suddenly dawned on me that this was totally different way of looking at plants. Seeing them as part of a system or a community was so completely different from the British mentality of collecting, labelling, and assembling individual plantings. Many British readers of the book unfortunately never understood Hansen's approach. Whatever its drawbacks in the hands of less creative followers, or maybe those outside Bavaria trying to apply it without critical thought, the "Hansen system" nevertheless proved a milestone in thinking about planting design.

Personal contacts between gardeners nearly always result in an exchange of plants. Two British plantsmen, Joe Sharman and Alan Leslie, had visited Hummelo and been with Piet to visit Ernst Pagels. They traded many plants, and since Alan later worked at the Royal Horticultural Society Garden at Wisley, he was able to pass on to Piet a new red astrantia, 'Ruby Wedding.' Normally off-white, astrantias are a genus whose appeal was mainly to the sophisticated gardener, but when they became available in red, their appeal widened dramatically. Piet was able to use them in his own breeding program, from which he named a red-toned seed-strain 'Claret,' and a pink cultivar 'Roma.'

The Garden Takes Shape

By 1993 the front garden at Hummelo had been laid down as trial beds for ten years. There were some yew pillars that gave it structure, but this was essentially a very functional space. The Netherlands is of course famously flood-prone, and this area is no exception. In 1993 a particularly disastrous flood covered the area for more than a week. "We lost eighty percent of our plants," Piet remembers. Having been forced to reconsider how he used the space, Piet decided to replant the area as a show garden. The front part of the garden was filled with imported soil, an existing circular pond was planted up, and the whole area given a strong central

Hedges in winter.

axis. Lammert van den Barg owned some land in the village; Piet rented some ground from him and moved some of his stock plants there, as well as many trial plants and seedlings he wanted to grow. From these seedlings he began to make his own selections. There was another important reason for moving plants out of the front garden. As Piet explains, "because the front garden became a show garden we needed space for the amount of plants we planned to propagate."

The front garden now had a clear central axis, although this initially could not be seen by visitors. At that time they would arrive by a small side entrance to find themselves on a brick path that took them diagonally across a modest-sized patch of lawn. Straight ahead of them was a large cherry tree, a survivor among several that attested to the land's days as a working farm. To one side was a border, with a depth of around 16 feet (5 meters); in some ways it was quite conventional in that the tallest plants were at the back and shortest at the front. Planted in 1993, it has been largely left untouched, a strong reminder of Piet's earlier design style. Reaching the end of this path, one turned a corner. At that point, the central axis of the garden would have been visible. The central path, however, was broken up by three beds, each an off-centered ellipse. There was symmetry, but symmetry with a twist—I overheard British art critic Roy Strong exclaim that it was "wonky baroque" on a visit a few years later. The middle bed held a mix of perennials and a few shrubs, but the first and the third were filled with silver-leaved *Stachys byzantina* 'Big Ears' and a few clumps of orange-flowered *Hemerocallis* 'Pardon Me.' Piet did confess once that he had put *Asarum europaeum* in there as ground cover, a decision he soon realized was "silly" as it could not cope with the sun. This was replaced with the *Stachys*.

Perennial planting filled the bulk of the side areas of the front garden, although this spread out rather more than would have happened in the borders of an English garden. Narrow brick paths acted as routes through places where the borders bulged out the most. For short distances, it was possible to walk through perennials, but otherwise one looked at them from the lawn. To one side was—and indeed still is—the hedge Piet famously clipped into curving forms. He dubbed it the "dragon's back hedge," and said it represented the skyline of the woodland across the road that existed at that time. In a mixed country hedge, each shrub got its own individual treatment, making it seem an irregular series of curves; in the winter the outlines of the trunk and branches were silhouetted. At the far end was the line of four yew hedges, cut to form what could best be described as curtains. Each was the same width, but their tops dipped up and down to form waves.

This was the state in which I first saw the garden, in August 1994. I visited on the same day as Eva Gustavsson, a lecturer in planting design from the landscape department of the Swedish University of Agricultural Sciences. At the time, I had not realized just how new the Hummelo garden was. It was my last major garden visit of the season—that year was momentous for me as I had been in Brazil in February, visiting Roberto Burle Marx in Rio de Janeiro (sadly, he was to die later that year), and then in a number of the most innovative public park plantings in Germany in June and July.

By this time, the nursery area on the rear side of the house was well established and ornamented with several young silver pear trees and some trompe l'oeil obelisks and statues. *Digitalis ferruginea* had sown itself into brick pavers; I remember being fascinated by that forest of narrow-spired seed heads. Plants for sale in half-liter or liter containers were arranged in rows, with shade lovers nearer the house and under mesh. Plants were not organized alphabetically—on purpose. As Piet explains, "I was afraid that in the period the plants were not in flower the customers would put them back among other varieties of the same plant." As with many other Dutch and German nurseries, customers wrote their own labels; strips of blanks and pencils were provided by Anja on arrival.

At the rear were rows of mother plants for propagating, in narrow rectangular beds about 5 feet (1.5 meters) wide. These were not organized in any obvious way, but each variety was very clearly marked with a big wooden label. At the very back some climbers, such as wisteria and celastrus, grew up metal supports. Beyond, fields of rich grass and dairy cattle stretched to the horizon. This whole stock plant area was not consciously designed, but with its almost random planting of perennials it looked liked a giant herbaceous border, or series of borders—a fact commented on by many visitors.

Meeting Piet then was a good way to end what had been a very adventurous year for me. He seemed to be one of the very few people

Voorkom beschadiging.
eerst kiezen, dan pakken.

who brought together clear design skills and plantsmanship. Burle Marx had also been one of a small number who seemed to combine those skills in one person, but there have been few others. James van Sweden and Wolfgang Oehme, partners I was to meet in 1996 in the U.S., brought both qualities together in a business relationship, even if by that time Wolfgang's plant selection had become increasingly dogmatic and conservative.

I had done a lot of traveling in 1994, and had been particularly inspired by the work of German planting designers, in particular those working in the Hansen tradition; with a plant palette largely familiar to me, they nevertheless used plants in much freer way than I was used to seeing in Britain. Their effect, I have always said, looks midway between a wildflower meadow and a conventional (i.e. British) herbaceous border. Their work had a sound scientific basis and related strongly to natural plant communities, both of which I liked. It was also about public space, which appealed to me politically; although I have had my fair share of working for wealthy clients, like many in the design profession, I have often wished the masses could share in what I do rather than a small, charmed circle. However, the German plantings came with a big drawback. All were made for large public parks. Each was the legacy of a summer-long garden show, part of whose purpose was urban regeneration through the creation of quality public space, with adventurous planting usually playing a prominent part. Much of this planting involved well-known designers working with nurseries to create perennial plantings for the long term. With the exception of one, Hermannshof (which in fact had *not* been part of a garden show), their scale was far larger than anything a private gardener could hope to achieve. In addition, despite a lot of research, I was unable to find any private gardeners influenced by this public work and hardly any designers seemed interested in applying their principles to the domestic garden.

Piet's ability to work as a designer, but with a clear focus on plants and planting, was strongly akin to my own interests. Working with a broadly similar plant palette to the German practitioners', and very aware of the beauty of natural habitats, Piet seemed to offer a version of the new thinking that was also realistic about the limits of the spaces it could occupy. His clipped woody plants anchored what he did in seasonal continuity and structure, and yet were radically different from anything else I had seen. The early 1990s, we must remember, were the time in Britain when the Arts and Crafts garden—so clearly exemplified by Vita Sackville-West and Harold Nicholson's Sissinghurst and Lawrence Johnston's Hidcote—were thought of as the height of what a garden should be, or indeed could be. The balance they achieved between formal structures and almost unkempt borders of burgeoning perennials was held to be the core of their success. Meeting Piet and seeing his gardens showed me that there were other ways of achieving the same balance. Later, I learned that this structural element was influenced by Mien Ruys and her Bauhaus/modernist background.

On subsequent visits to Piet and Anja, which tended to be at least annual, I have witnessed many changes, but they have tended to be incremental. They also quite logically paralleled what Piet was doing in his career. As he became more confident with perennials and began to use more grasses in different ways, they took over. They gradually ate away at the lawn turf and the clipped woody plants.

The nursery area and front garden experienced only minor changes until the mid-2000s. One large change, however, came in July 1997 when the old cherry tree in the front garden had to be felled. The ground beneath was dry and nutrient starved as places beneath trees often are. Piet replaced it with a bold circular bed, which at the time he called "the necklace." A low wall of red brick fronted a retainer for soil around 2 feet (60 centimeters) high, but interspersed with a clipped yew every few meters. The bed was planted with *Miscanthus sinensis* 'Malepartus' growing out of a mass of *Carex muskingumensis*. The effect is almost evergreen, as the *Carex* greens up rapidly in the spring (and indeed in some winters it stays green).

Behind the house stand two buildings, of brick and dark-treated wood restored from the jumble of sheds left over from when this was a farmyard. For the Oudolfs they served as centers for warmth, coffee, and hospitality for nursery and garden visitors and guests. Between them and the house are two square beds, which in the early years held a few perennials, bulbs, occasional annuals, and some clematis climbing up iron supports. In the late 1990s they acquired the plant selection that still dominates them today. This reflects the range of plants that began to interest Piet at this time: many North American species such

Sporobolus heterolepis, a prairie grass Oudolf first encountered in America and still uses extensively in his designs.

as *Veronicastrum virginicum, Amsonia hubrichtii*, and most notably the grasses *Panicum virgatum* and *Sporobolus heterolepis*. Today, the big clumps of these plants that remain are a clear and powerful indication of their longevity and value for gardens and landscapes in Northern Europe.

The beauty of the garden at Hummelo was not to everyone's taste, however. Veteran German garden photographer Jürgen Becker visited for the first time in the autumn of 1995 and commented to Piet that there was "not so much in flower." Piet also recalls that, similarly, photographer Marijke Heuff didn't photograph much there, presumably because "she didn't feel at home." In July 1996, Britain's BBC flagship television program, *Gardeners' World*, came to film it with presenter Stephen Lacey. Piet remembers that "he did not understand our planting at that time, he was new to it." I think he may actually have understood more than he was letting on—he was very supportive of Brita von Schoenaich and her then-business-partner Tim Reece, who were instrumental in putting on the Perennial Perspectives conferences at Kew Gardens in 1994 and 1997. He also wrote very positively about German perennial planting in several magazine articles.

Attracting the Public's Attention

In 1994 Piet designed a border in the Utrecht Botanical Garden—this was to be his first public planting. It measured 13,000 square feet (1,200 square meters), and its shape was traditional, designed to run alongside a path. Nevertheless, it was a golden opportunity for him to show off his work to a wider audience. He had visited the garden one day and met the hortulanus (i.e. garden director) at the time, Wiert Nieuman, and in conversation, agreed to make the planting. Wiert remembers that "in the autumn of that year we prepared the plot, we made the paths, and then we waited on a reaction from Piet … at the end of February I had still heard nothing from him. A little bit anxious, I phoned him with the question if he had forgotten us … No, not at all, he answered. He said, 'come with your Volkswagen pickup to my nursery, we'll fill it with plants, and I'll drive with you to Utrecht. Then we can make the border.' So I did. There was no plan, no sketch … Piet laid the plants on the field and I and my staff planted the perennials. Unbelievable, all he did without a plan on paper!!"

Wiert reports that "over the years, the border has been sometimes dug up and planted again, but still it is an Oudolf border, and we still are very happy with it." Piet expresses surprise that the border has lasted. "I am not in favor of keeping gardens so long—I am not Mien Ruys—but I suppose they want to keep it as heritage." His attitude to preserving gardens is a very phlegmatic one, very different from that of many in the garden world, who are anxious to preserve anything even remotely notable. "Sometimes I have seen clients with an old Mien Ruys garden, but I cannot see anything remaining there of her ... people have to move on, gardens have to change," he says.

Piet's number of private garden commissions began to build during this time. One was for photographer Walter Herfst and his family, who first met Piet when he was sent to Hummelo to shoot Piet's portrait for a magazine. "It was an eye-opener" Herfst said, "and I liked photographing beauty after all the journalistic work I do." He also commissioned Piet to redesign his garden in Rotterdam, which had an average long, thin, town-garden shape as well as a small wooden office at its end.

Another somewhat larger—but by no means big—garden commission was for Klaus and Ulrike Thews. The couple had bought a 150-year-old traditional cottage and a small patch of land in Germany's northernmost province, Schleswig-Holstein, as a weekend retreat in 1981. Klaus recalls, "Ulrike always gardened, even if only on the balcony in Hamburg ... In 1994, she saw a magazine article about Piet Oudolf, so she phoned him and asked him whether he could help with a bed ... Piet understood what she meant, and we drove over to see him ... it was a quick decision. We asked him for some plans. He asked us to each write a wish list. Ulrike wanted a place to sit and inhale the beauty of the flowers, I wanted a tension between clear formal features and abundant perennial borders." Later, they decided to retire and live full time there, so they built a modern extension onto the house. In 2004 they got Piet back to extend the garden and make larger perennial plantings. Klaus recalls how in "two days in May, he helped to plant 1,200 perennials."

Another important project from these years was John Coke's property at Bury Court in England. John had bought a former farmhouse and its associated buildings after Jenkyn Place vineyard, which had belonged to his parents, had been sold after their death. John emphasises that "it was not our plan to have Piet design the garden, the idea was just to make some simple beds as display beds for the nursery ... we had a rather mad collection—some alpines, tender plants, trees, all sorts, not much that was in his range—we had just dug out the old yard and were poised to do our beds when Piet came to visit. He asked whether he could make us a drawing. I had not thought of asking him anything like that at all, but then I thought, why not? It forced us to change our whole list, so we started growing all these grasses and tall perennials."

Piet recalls that John had wanted him to cut borders out of the old concrete, but he refused and said it must all go. "I did not want to make just one flowing garden, but to make different places ... a gravel garden for the first time ... and a knot garden inspired by Rosemary Verey." John remembers how "Piet had a strict and stern view about things, and when he did his plan, that was that—take it or leave it, more or less." The problem remained, however, of how to integrate the eclectic range of plants that John grew for the nursery into that plan. John recalls it as a kind of compromise: "His one concession to us was that we could plant *our* kind of plants around the edge." This was a solution Piet used again at Scampston Hall—the "Plantsman's Walk" around the perimeter came about for much the same reason. He has always recognized that there are certain plants people like to grow, collector's or connoisseur's plants, which need special conditions, extra care, or which simply do not fit into his design style. Growing them in a special, visually segregated area where they can be appreciated but will not interfere with the main design is his favored solution.

Bury Court resulted in two innovations for Piet: one was the gravel garden, the other the *Deschampsia* meadow. The *Deschampsia* meadow was a very successful design concept on paper, but in this location it had its problems (discussed later). I remember talking to Piet at the time about the gravel garden, which seemed an almost obvious thing to include in the sheltered, south-facing location. He was cautious about it, however, and although it proved very successful it has not been repeated—the plant range needed to create one is simply so very different in character to the usual Oudolf palette. Perhaps it was a concession to the site, to John, or to a distinctive planting style that works very well in the mild British climate.

Views of Bury Court in Hampshire, England—Oudolf's first commission in the United Kingdom.

CLIPPING

An aspect of two of the first of Piet's British commissions (Bury Court and Scampston), which not everyone remarked immediately, was the role of clipped woody plants in his early work. Since then, however, he has used them much less. The modernist/Mien Ruys garden style of Piet's younger days, with its emphasis on contemporary clipping, has simply worn off over time. From a Dutch perspective, dropping them seemed an obvious development—their style had been taken so far that perhaps it could not be taken much further. Piet's use of it may also have been skilful, but he recognized that it was not unique. For the rest of us however, this is not the case—we still have a lot to learn. Clipping woody plants, in most countries, is an extraordinarily unadventurous undertaking. The range of species used tends to be narrow, and the unimaginative fixation with using them to create perpendicular frameworks is ubiquitous. For many of us in the 1990s, the sight of Piet's blocks of clipped box or yew were a revelation. Bury Court (1996) is a good example—a great fat button of box acts as a hinge on a stone path, marking a shift in its direction, and a circle of box with a spiral twist sits like an abstract sculpture outside one of the old barns. From the late 1990s on, it seemed that clipped yew, beech, or box were mostly likely to appear in Piet's work in smaller gardens only, where something was needed to differentiate space, such as in the Thews garden (first laid out 1996), or the Boon garden (2000).

The privately owned Thews garden in Schleswig-Holstein, Germany, first designed by Oudolf in 1996 and extended in 2006.

The Boon garden in The Netherlands, designed in 2000.

One of the last gardens to feature significant clipping was Scampston Hall (1999). Aerial photographs used on its website show clearly what is not always so obvious to the visitor on the ground: there is a belt on the outside of perennial-dominated planting, but the inside area is taken up with several gardens with clipped plants.

For those in climates where summer temperatures limit flowering perennials, either through drought or heat, clipped woody plants have a lot to offer. Particularly in the American South, with its enormous range of evergreen shrubs, for example; or China; or Mediterranean climates. The modernism-averse British have even finally paid them some attention. Tom Stuart-Smith, for example, has used beech columns extensively in his work. Clipping remains popular with many garden owners, and we are fortunate that we do have designers who continue to try to push the boundaries with it, such as Nico Kloppenborg in Friesland, a northern Dutch province. For many of us, though, clipped forms can only be considered a backdrop and contrast for perennials!

The fee was then called into question. Conscious that the design had been his idea, and that this client was also a friend, Piet refused to invoice John for his time. He only requested payment for the plants, which had come from Hummelo. John insisted that he pay something. Piet pointed to the rug on the floor of John's office, a very nice antique Caucasian. "I'll take that," he said.

Perennial Perspectives

A series of annual conferences titled "Perennial Perspectives" was a very distinctive feature of the first half of the 1990s. The concept had really started with an event organized in 1992 in Sweden; Rob Leopold then came up with the title and an informal movement to continue them began. In 1994, a young German landscape architect and teacher of planting design, Brita von Schoenaich, organized a conference at Kew Gardens in London called "New Trends in Planting Design." The emphasis was on Germany, but there was a Dutch delegation present, including Piet and of course, an ebullient Rob Leopold. Among the speakers was Rosemarie Weisse, who had been part of the group to create a spectacular "steppe" dry landscape planting at an International Garden Show in Munich's Westpark in 1983. (This particular planting made a big impact on all of us who saw it; I shall never forget my first sight of it.) For those of us who had heard rumors of interesting ecology-oriented plantings happening in Germany, this was a fantastic opportunity to find out more and make contacts. To set the seal of approval on what was, for some, the revolutionary and disturbing idea that British gardeners could learn from other countries—and even from Germans—Beth Chatto gave a presentation. Without any links to the German practitioners of the perennial-focused planting style, Beth had for years been promoting its British equivalent, the idea (so obvious to us now) that plant selection should be based on habitat preferences. Beth also spoke German and had for years been making visits to her friend Helen von Stein Zeppelin and her nursery in Baden-Württemberg. On one occasion she had been helping out by propagating perennials, and at the next bench was a young man who would go on to become very prominent in the movement: Cassian Schmidt.

Another speaker was James Hitchmough, then a lecturer at the Scottish Agricultural University at Auchincruive on the southwest coast of Scotland. This was the first time many of us had heard of him, though he went on to become one of the most innovative thinkers and productive researchers in the field of perennials, specifically their use in public space and in lower-maintenance planting schemes. Like many others, I remember the Geordie accent[3] and a very sharp sense of humor. Presentations by James were the highlight of many future such events, and he put on a number of highly effective conferences with colleague Nigel Dunnett at the University of Sheffield in future years.

The Kew conference came at an extraordinarily good time for me. Within weeks, I was due to drive to Bratislava to visit my girlfriend, Jo Eliot, who had just got a job at a university in the newly independent Slovak Republic. My journey would take me through Germany, so I was able to include visits to some planting projects along the way. My arrival at the Westpark in Munich in late May 1994 was a revelation for its dreamlike use of familiar garden plants in expansively unfamiliar ways. I hurriedly set about trying to reclaim the German I had learned at school.

The Perennial Perspectives conference in 1995 was held in Freising, the small Bavarian town that is home to the Sichtungsgarten Weihenstephan and the Weihenstephan-Triesdorf University of Applied Sciences; it is where many of the best horticulture and landscape professionals are trained. Each PP conference included a tour for the conference speakers and a few other guests. Piet joined the tour this year, which was when he met Stefan Mattson, along with the leading German landscape architect of the time and an innovator in large-scale planting design, Heiner Luz. Anita Fischer, a landscape architect who lived and practiced in Freising, was also present. Anita went on to launch a uniquely elegant garden show modeled both on Bingerden and Courson, the Freisinger Gartentage. Speakers that year included Piet, who gave a lecture entitled "A New Concept in Using Perennials in Public Spaces and Gardens," alongside Rune Bengtsson, Urs Walser, and Hein Koningen.

A memory I have of the Freising conference illustrates one of the tensions inherent in the nascent movement. A young researcher, Yvonne Boison from the University of Paderborn, in Germany, was discussing research on insect populations in urban vegetation. Partway through she was heckled by Gabriella Pape, a German landscape designer who has never made any secret of her dislike for the Hansen approach. She

Rob Leopold with Jacqueline van der Kloet, top. Brita von Schoenaich, Anja Oudolf, and British garden designer Julie Toll, below.

shouted something along the lines of "never mind the insects, what about the people?" Those with a perspective strongly driven by a passion for nature or a political interpretation of ecology have often expressed support for planting styles that privilege native species and biodiversity over ornamentation; but on the other hand the viewpoint that landscapes serve only human interests now seems very old-fashioned. Many practitioners argue that planting design can be for the benefit of humanity *and* nature. The following speaker was, again, James Hitchmough. With Nigel Dunnett, he later came up with the concept of "enhanced nature" as a way of reconciling human needs and biodiversity.

"Perennial Perspectives," notes Rosie Atkins, "were events where everyone was looking for a new philosophy, new ways of doing things … they were incredibly refreshing. To us, it was a movement like the surrealists or the Bauhaus." By the 1996 event, held in Arnhem, about half an hour's drive from Hummelo, there was the sense that a true movement was underway. That event lasted for two days and was followed, some months later, by the publication of a book of conference documents. Piet spoke on "Perennials as Building Elements," and showed a series of images that identified some of the key perennials he was using, organized by seasonal interest.

My book *The New Perennial Garden* was also published in 1996. Its London publisher Frances Lincoln, who was to die at the all-too-young age of fifty-five some five years later, gave it its title. The book concentrated on trying to bring an understanding of the German approach to planting design to an English-speaking audience. It stayed in print for many years, went through several editions, and was much appreciated in college courses. Although it did not cover Piet's work, it probably played a role in preparing the ground for him in the English-speaking world. As Charles Quest-Ritson said in the *Garden Design Journal*, "One of the earliest champions was Noël Kingsbury, who had studied the German models and immediately understood their potential in the British Isles. His book … and his gardens at Cowley, now lost, were catalysts; their importance cannot be over-emphasised." He goes on to mention Dan Pearson and Christopher Bradley-Hole as other British designers who "were quick to realize the possibilities."[4]

Despite the professional success of these events, the symposium or conference was not a particularly popular format in the garden world, at least in Europe. Perennial Perspectives ground to a halt after another gathering at Kew in 1997, basically because the members of the organizing committee were too busy with their own professional lives. We did not know that this would be the last symposium; indeed at the time, the thinking was that there would be another, in the U.S. The second Kew Perennial Perspectives featured some American speakers for the first time: Wolfgang Oehme and Neil Diboll, a very engaging and entertaining "prairie restorationist" from Wisconsin. Oehme, much respected for his plant knowledge, was famously a terrible lecturer, and this occasion was no different from any other in that respect, as he stood with his back to the audience for much of the time, preferring to address his photographs.

Sweden: The Turning Point

Contact with Sweden came early in Piet's career. Although Swedish garden culture was arguably at a low ebb by the late 1980s and early 1990s, there were a small number of academics interested in planting in the departments of landscape and of horticulture at the Swedish Agricultural University (SLU) at Alnarp, just outside the southernmost major city in the country, Malmö. Kenneth Lorentzon was one. He was a man with the passion for plants that was more typical of a British plantsman. He had been at university with Stefan Mattson, who went into public green space management and who later played a crucial role in launching Piet's career as a designer of public spaces. Rune Bengtsson was another. Mattson thinks it was Rune who really discovered Piet: "He organized a seminar in Alnarp where some Dutch people came and he did two courses on perennials in Enköping for the staff. As thanks for my help he said he would take me to Holland and show me some interesting things there."

Eva Gustavsson, also an Alnarp faculty member, explained that despite the poverty of contemporary Swedish planting design, "we had a big connection with Germany and the habitat planting, we have been raised with it ... then we were influenced by England and then this combination of Germany and England in the Dutch experience." She met Piet at a conference held at Alnarp in January 1992, organized by

Rune and Evor Bucht under the banner of MOVIUM, a landscape think tank. She took an interest in his work and was also researching planting design at the time.

The theme of the Alnarp conference was Dutch planting design. Rune and others had been in contact with Dutch colleagues since the late seventies, largely regarding projects looking at the use of native species in planting design. They had known Hein Koningen and Rob Leopold for a long time, and some English people: Chris Baines, who started the wildlife garden movement with his very influential book *How to Make a Wildlife Garden* (1984), and Robert Tregay, who at the time was an influential voice in developing plant-rich urban landscapes. On one trip, while in Amsterdam, Rune and Evor popped into the design bookshop Architectura & Natura to try to find out what else might be going on. They found a copy of *Droomplanten* and so became aware of Piet and Henk, and discovered other books with photography by Marijke Heuff that made the misty, romantic most of naturalistic plantings. The trip also enabled them to track down Coen Jansen.

The MOVIUM conference helped persuade a publisher to translate *Dreamplants* as *Drömplantor: den nya generationen perenner* in 1995; it was the book's first foreign edition. This was indeed an accolade, as Swedish publishers at the time were notoriously reluctant to take on foreign garden books, or indeed to publish much on gardening at all. Eva Gustavsson describes the book as having "had an enormous impact."

Possibly the most significant single event in Piet's life as a designer began with a joke and a slight misunderstanding. It happened in 1995, on the tour of parks and gardens in southern Germany that was part of the Freising conference. Piet was sitting on the coach next to Stefan Mattson, who at the time was superintendent of parks in the small city of Enköping, in central Sweden. Stefan remembers how "he showed me his catalogue, and I asked him what perennials would be good for public places ... he said everything is good for public places, so I thought I would make a little joke. I said he should come to Enköping and he could make a design for a planting in a park, I didn't actually mean to commission him ... he became very serious and said he would like to do that."

Almost a dare, Mattson's decision to let Piet loose in central Sweden at a latitude of 59°N was a bold one. In retrospect it was a turning point

because it was Piet's first commission to work on a public space outside The Netherlands. It brought Piet a great deal of very beneficial publicity. The impact on Sweden was also considerable. Although there had been a period between the 1920s and 1940s when natural-style planting and perennials had been popular, during the 1950s there had been a turning away from diverse planting in favor of a very functional style. A time of major urban development saw a strongly collectivist ethos prevail: landscape architects were working on public housing projects, parks, and children's play areas using only a limited range of plants. Private gardening simply went out of fashion, and designers lost interest in the domestic garden. Many nurseries often stocked little more than conifers.

Enköping, however, had become something of a garden gem in Sweden since Stefan Mattson had taken over as director in 1981. Among his first tasks was reviewing the procurement and planting of 30,000 bedding plants every year: "I felt that a great amount of money was being spent on plantings in parks that the public did not necessarily like, and meanwhile the rest of the park that was not covered with beds would be filled with large areas of mown grass. I thought I could use the money spent on the bedding and on cutting the grass to create larger, colorful areas for the public to enjoy—using a different approach."[5] With only an average budget for public landscape management, Stefan set about implementing a number of innovative schemes to improve the town's green places for both people and biodiversity. A particular innovation were the "pocket parks," small neighborhood parks that relied heavily on perennials and that were maintained to a standard specification. By the early 1990s, work in Enköping was attracting an increasing number of visitors and attention from the landscape and horticulture professions.

After commissioning Piet to create a large-scale perennial planting for a park, Stefan selected a relatively high-profile area, which people could see on their way to work, and requested a "labyrinth-like effect." The name *Droomparken* (Dreampark) was settled on, after the title of the book. Most of the plants Piet wanted to use were not available in Sweden at the time, so the Hummelo nursery supplied them. Stefan recalls that "everything arrived marked, so crates would have numbers corresponding to particular areas in the planting. It was easy to see where everything went. I said to the staff, we need to get a contractor to help,

Ulf Nordfjell with Oudolf, Anja Oudolf, and Julie Toll.

but the staff wanted to do it themselves—and be paid overtime. The real work started in April 1996, and it was all planted by midsummer."

Possibly the most daunting factor was climate. Sub-zero temperatures for days on end in winter were common and the thermometer could plunge as low as -22°F (-30°C). Stefan asked Rune Bengtsson for advice; he suggested that many of the plants would need to be covered over in the winter. "But we did not have time to cover anything, so we just had to leave everything exposed," Stefan remembers. "We decided it would be like a lesson for us—we would have to learn by repetition what worked." Happily, in spring they found that very few plants had to be replaced. Grasses proved the most problematic, as the smaller plants failed to overwinter. Stefan's previous experience had taught him about reliable perennials, which he calls base perennials, or "ones you can trust ... the next time you do something you can add some new things you want to try ... this time it was a lot more new things than we would normally try."

There were some problems, which Piet accepts. "I made mistakes with some short-lived plants, and the *Eupatorium* and *Filipendula* flowered together because of the short growing season with its long days of midsummer sunshine, but that was a nice mistake—they look so good and so fresh together. That would never happen at home. *Persicaria* was also a mistake, as it has superficial roots and so can suffer freezing. There were problems also with the Japanese anemones (*Anemone* x *hybrida* varieties), which were not sufficiently cold-tolerant." The great success was the "salvia river" feature, which has been a particular favorite with the public; Piet recalls the origin of the idea as "an indoor show I had seen with lavender. I realized that with three colors of salvia, you can create a sense of depth."

Stefan was therefore largely vindicated in his choice of Piet and his plant selection. By 2003, in tandem with some local redevelopment and effective lobbying of the town's politicians, the Dreampark was expanded to a total of 42,000 square feet (4,000 square meters). Enköping as a town hosts over 200 tour groups a year, and as many visit its parks (which helps to pay for maintenance, of course) a great many people have been introduced to the world of perennial growing. Eva Gustavsson reckons that "Dreampark had an enormous influence on Sweden. Piet is a garden star here. Almost everyone in gardening in Sweden knows his name."

In 2007 Stefan decided to move on and took a job in Stockholm with Sweden's largest housing company, Svenska Bostäder, as head gardener. In 2010, he was able to commission Piet to design a 64,500-square-foot (6,000-square-meter) park in a working-class suburb, Skärholmen, as part of an urban regeneration project. Other projects in Sweden include a 17,000-square-foot (1,600-square-meter) planting on a promontory into the Baltic at Solvesborg, a town on the southern coast. Eva Gustavsson reports that when the park director Kristina Höijer asked the town council to fund it, she had to face the fact that none of them were gardeners and did not know who Piet was; by making a comparison between Piet and internationally-known footballers like Ronaldo or Beckham, and by garnering the support of the town architect, she got the necessary money.

Dreampark, the other Oudolf projects, and of course *Dreamplants* the book seem to have kick-started a true revival in planting design in Sweden. The plant selection promoted by the projects in particular has proved a powerful stimulus for the use of a much wider range of perennials. Other practitioners have also been able to ride a wave of enthusiasm for perennials and their use in the country's very democratic public spaces. One example from the coastal city of Gothenburg—which has a mild climate, relatively speaking—is the way that Mona Holmberg and Ulf Strindberg have used vast swathes of a very wide range of perennials around housing projects in the city, even supplying interpretation boards with weatherproof planting plans, which astonish visitors by their mere survival in some of the rougher neighborhoods. As Rune Bengtsson wrote in a foreword for the second Swedish edition of *Dreamplants*, "Piet's work is one of the biggest [garden] trend breaks in the twentieth century." The impact on the plant selection being grown and sold by Swedish nurseries has also been considerable. A very wide variety of perennials is now available.

Originally a ceramicist, Ulf Nordfjell has become the most famous native Swedish garden and landscape designer, and he works very much within the naturalistic and perennial-rich ethos. In a typically public-spirited Swedish way, he divides his time between private practice and working for companies designing public landscapes. He has been the lead architect of two very successful garden shows in Sweden, in 1998 at the

Rosendal Garden in Stockholm and in 2008 in Gothenburg for the city's garden society, which have helped raise the profile of garden-making and quality planting design. For the latter event, Piet made a small planting and led a seminar.

Grasses

"How can these jewels of the garden have been virtually ignored for so long?" asked Karl Foerster in 1957 in *Einzug der Gräser und Farne in die Gärten* (*The Introduction of Grasses and Ferns into the Garden*). Foerster played a major role in popularizing these plants, which had up until then not been considered beautiful or appropriate for gardens. Piet has of course followed. Grasses were certainly not unknown, just under-appreciated; articles about *Miscanthus* appeared in British garden magazines in the late ninteenth century and a handful of species were occasionally used, but during the twentieth century their use tended to be limited to very naturalistic plantings. During the 1980s, Foerster's pupil Ernst Pagels grew a number of grass genera, raising at least twenty-four new cultivars of *Miscanthus sinensis* and one *Molinia*. The Pagels nursery at Leer was only about two hours' drive from Hummelo, so it was almost inevitable that he and his grasses would play a role in Piet's developing design palette. Piet first discovered the value of grasses, however, at Peter zur Linden's nursery in Osnabrück, in Germany, but it was Ernst Pagels who was the source of most plants. He, in turn, came to Hummelo, where he expressed great happiness at what he saw.

"I was already interested in grasses," says Piet, "but not in borders—using them either separately or with robust perennials." As his design style developed during the 1980s and 1990s, he became more confident in using them integrated into plantings that also featured a wide range of flowering perennials. "Germany" he says, "was the best source for grasses, we had connections with many botanic gardens. We knew Hans Simon, we got a lot from him, some from Urs Walser, some came from England." Later, while working on the Lurie Garden in Chicago, Piet was introduced to North American grasses, particularly the genera: *Panicum, Schizachyrium*, and *Sporobolus*. All grow well in Northern Europe.

Two of Oudolf's favorite grasses, *Pennisetum viridescens*, left, and *Schizachyrium scoparium*, above.

A key development in crystallizing Piet's thinking about grasses was a collaboration on a book about them. Michael King, who had worked as the secretary of Kew Gardens—a rather quaint title that means he was secretary to the Board of Trustees and also head of the finance and administration department of the Royal Botanic Gardens—moved to Amsterdam "as a refugee from Mrs. Thatcher." He started to visit Hummelo. "I discovered Piet just as someone running a nursery," he told me. "We became friends ... I wanted to write a book about grasses because I had been fascinated by what James van Sweden and Wolfgang Oehme were doing [in the U.S.], and there was nothing written about their approach and nothing decent written about grasses. Once Piet and I started talking about grasses, he offered his photographs for the book—I suggested he cowrite it, but he did not want to. After a year or more, he changed his mind. I had admired the plants, and had seen what people in Germany were doing, but I had not necessarily grown them. He had that experience."

"For the grasses book," Michael recalls, "Piet had to explain what he was doing for the first time. He had a concept about silhouettes, but otherwise I felt he had not refined his thinking. He talked about the winter landscape and how grasses were very important to that. The only thing we disagreed about was a chapter on colored grasses. He said, "we can't have that. I can't have a chapter on color ... it is the one thing that is completely unimportant with what I think you should do with grasses." In fact, the book did not ignore color, but Piet's point echoed a deeper concern, that a grass's structure was the all-important issue.

As happens so often, Michael's main obstacle was convincing a publisher. In the end Terra, a major Dutch publisher, took it on, but was unenthusiastic about foreign editions. Apparently I introduced Michael to Erica Hunningher, who at the time was a highly influential editor in British garden publishing—I had forgotten, but Michael reminded me. "In the end, my grasses book spawned more than gardening ideas," Michael recalls, "My publisher in Holland ended up having a personal relationship with Erica." The book clearly hit the market at the right time, and was published in both English as *Gardening with Grasses* at the same time as in Dutch, as *Prachtig Gras*, in 1996. Henk Gerritsen translated Michael's English into Dutch; a German edition soon followed. A launch party in Amsterdam was attended by Ernst Pagels, and what Michael

Persicaria amplexicaulis 'Firedance,' above, and *Actaea* 'Queen of Sheba,' below; both plants figure prominently in Oudolf's later designs.

calls "his entourage" of family and friends, which everyone saw as the ultimate seal of approval.

The book is unusual in that it concentrates heavily on the uses to which grasses can be put, although an A-Z of species is also included. Grasses are considered specimen plants, and as potential components of meadows, borders, and even containers. Particularly appreciated by readers I have spoken to was material on combining grasses with perennials, but also a lot of new thinking on how grasses could be combined with a range of plants, including large-leaved perennials, umbellifers, and autumn-flowering perennials. There was a whole section on umbellifers, members of what is now called the *Apiaceae* by botanists, but which were once known as the *Umbelliferae*—the cow parsley and Queen Anne's lace family. There were plant lists and suggested combinations. Autumn and winter interest got a particular focus. It was, in other words, a very hard-working book for gardeners and designers. And, crucially, for the first time, Piet was forced to outline his planting design philosophy. The volume made a particular impact on Roy Diblik, a grower and designer in Wisconsin. "In 1998," he remembers, "I was given a copy of the book. I thought it was just another gardening book, and I left it on the passenger seat of the pickup for a while. But when I looked at it properly it left me in tears. No one had written like this before, about the interplay with perennials. It really engaged me like no other book had."

Breeding New Plants

A great many people in the nursery trade end up naming their own plants, and Piet was no exception. "We found a seedling one time," he told me. "It was from *Gaura lindheimeri*, and flowered an extremely long time, but sterile. We named it 'Whirling Butterflies,' and it's still in the trade." In particular, many plants grown from seed will show natural variation, with the possibility that one individual may stand out as superior or different in some way, and be worth picking out, naming, and propagating. A more deliberate creation of new varieties can be done if large numbers of seedlings are planted out, with the express purpose of selecting the best forms, and then ruthlessly culling the rest.

An early success was *Salvia verticillata* 'Purple Rain,' a mysteriously dark form of a perennial very common in Eastern Europe. "It got us

Perennials that form a regular part of Oudolf's planting palette. From top left to below right: *Persicaria amplexicaulis* 'Firedance,' *Phlox divaricata* 'May Breeze,' *Sanguisorba menziesii* 'Wake Up,' *Salvia* 'Dear Anja,' *Salvia* 'Madeline,' *Sidalcea* 'Little Princess,' *Stachys* new selection, *Echinacea* 'Virgin,' and *Astrantia* 'Washfield.'

interested in doing our own work with seedlings. Because of it, we started to sow plants and make selections." Piet also recalls that the Sahin company, major seed producers in the south of the country, "grew thousands of plants, so after they had taken out what they wanted they let us take out what we liked for ourselves. They were happy to do let us do that—it was in the days before PBR." This stands for "Plant Breeders' Rights," a system that acts as a kind of patent. It enables originators of innovative plants to benefit from their foresight and their work—but it also had the effect of making growers more protective of potentially valuable genetic material.

Once he decided to move more systematically into plant breeding, Piet rented a small patch of land, about 43,000 square feet (4,000 square meters) in the village from Lammert, and grew thousands of seedlings. The plot was useful for stock plants too. He picked out potentially good new varieties, and in some cases was able to sell the unwanted wholesale, which helped pay for the breeding work. During the 1990s and early 2000s he managed to select around eighty cultivars that he thought worth naming. He also undertook some mass selection, which is a process of continually sowing batches of seed: good plants are picked out from a sowing, their seed sown, the best picked out from that generation, and so on until a particular distinctive characteristic is stabilized. "I did this with *Echinacea*," he recalls, "and with *Astrantia* 'Claret.' It took five or six years to get a good seed strain ... but it was almost ninety-nine percent true." He reckons his *Echinacea* selections, notable for their dark stems and flowers, are longer-lived than many available commercially.

Piet's work on *Echinacea* is interesting as well as potentially important. This North American perennial has become very popular. Its big, daisy-like flowers have a very high level of popular appeal, yet it has a poor record for longevity. Genetically predisposed to be short-lived, there is almost certainly also genetic variation in its lifespan. The 2000s saw a lot of breeding of *E. purpurea* with other *Echinacea* species, mostly in the U.S. This was aimed largely at the garden center trade. Some exciting color breaks—oranges and apricots—resulted, but the plants were mostly short-lived. For those wanting longer-lived plants, this breeding has not been of any use. We can only hope that someone picks up Piet's work on longevity.

Echinacea purpurea 'Fatal Attraction' in full bloom and in midwinter.

With *Monarda,* Piet wanted to increase the range of color as well as to select for resistance to mildew. He named his strains for signs of the zodiac or Native American tribes. In the end however, he had to face the fact that after a few years, the mildew fungus itself will inevitably evolve and affect the new varieties. We do have some good, vigorous cultivars in a wide range of colors as a result of his work, though. They are fantastically good bee plants and a good source of color before the main perennial season gets going in late summer; their seed heads withstand the winter well too.

The risk of breeding a good new variety is that its originator is liable to lose it very soon, when others in the business obtain it and start to propagate and sell it themselves. As Piet says, "we wanted to commercialize the plants we bred, and even without Plant Breeders' Rights we could sell a lot at the beginning." He enrolled some of his plants with a company called Multigrow, in which he was a partner, and who gave a 5 percent royalty for the first two years. "After two years, the plants were everywhere here. So we lost out." In 1998 Piet got together with two other growers and breeders of perennials to start a new company, Future Plants, to market their introductions and to protect their work through Plant Breeders' Rights and other novel forms of legal protection. The biggest clients were companies who were exporting to North America, so sometimes Piet would have the odd experience of "seeing plants of mine in production in America before Dutch nurseries were growing them ... Midwest Groundcovers and Dale Hendricks of North Creek would get these new plants into production so quickly ... I benefited much from this when I started to work in the U.S." Until the early 1990s, Dutch companies exporting to North America dealt in a wide range of cultivars but from a rather limited number of genera, notably *Astilbe, Hemerocallis,* and *Hosta.* "We had very different plants for them to choose from," Piet said, "so they were very keen to buy from us ... they loved our *Monardas.*" Rather than get involved in selling bare-root plants, Future Plants has concentrated on selling licenses to propagate. This reflected the decline in the global trade of bare-root plants; by the mid 2000s, the bare-root trade was replaced by selling either propagating material (such as unrooted cuttings) or the right to propagate agreed numbers of plants.

Astrantia 'Claret' and 'Roma' have been extremely successful as part of a whole suite of cultivars that have transformed *Astrantia* into an important garden perennial genus, at least for those of us in the cooler parts of Europe. *Sanguisorba* 'Tanna' is perhaps part of an even bigger achievement, as *Sanguisorba* were almost unknown as garden plants until Piet promoted them. Piet explains that " 'Tanna' was a strain from a Japanese botanical garden that we grew in the early eighties, when we ordered seeds from botanical garden seed lists." Piet has made selections of many other cultivars of this very useful summer flowering genus—which also has some of the best early summer foliage of any perennial. *Veronicastrum virginicum* 'Apollo' is the most widely distributed of Piet's several selections of a species that was no more than a connoisseur's plant before; now it is part of the core selection of any nursery trading in perennials. A prairie species, it encapsulates many qualities of "a good structure plant," as Piet would call it. It flowers in early to midsummer, and it keeps a fine vertical thrust right up until it is cut down in winter. *Eupatorium maculatum* 'Purple Bush' is a useful short, bushy form of a good late-summer perennial, though many find it too tall for their gardens. *Salvia verticillata* 'Purple Rain' was very popular for many years, but has not been seen so much of late despite having a very dark, very matte purple color that is quite unique. It has survived to a good age in some gardens, but its longevity has not been universal.

Fewer new plants come out of Hummelo now. As Piet says, "we stopped actively looking five years ago, but we still find new plants occasionally, like *Actaea* 'Queen of Sheba.' " This is a stunning, tall, branched hybrid, probably originating from a cross between *A. ramosa* 'Atropurpurea' and *A. dahurica*. Piet's achievements as a plant breeder have often not been realized by those who only see his design work. It is quite rare for a practicing designer to work in plant variety selection at all. In some ways, it seems odd that those involved in planting design pay so little attention to the development of new materials.

Monarda 'Ou Charm,' top, and *Astrantia major* 'Roma,' two plants Oudolf propagated and popularized.

Public Commissions

Major design commissions, from the first phone call to the last perennial being planted in the ground, can take years to complete. Following Piet's design of the garden at Bury Court, two other English commissions landed on his drawing board. Although they were very different, both were about creating gardens as visitor attractions. Gardening in general was beginning to go through something of a boom in Britain at the time, and so was tourism. As more people found themselves with the money to enjoy their leisure time, especially the retired generation, the demand grew for places to go. These had been quite clearly defined in the U.K.: stately homes, castles, and gardens. The 1990s saw a change, however, to something more general and multifaceted. "Heritage" was a key buzzword in these years, but many people had a thirst for quality contemporary design that was not being satisfied. There was a growing recognition that, to get visitors to a place, the management needed to take account of the fact that the interests of a couple, a family, or a group of friends were different from those of the older generation. Building a new garden as part of an existing "heritage" attraction was one way to entice, entertain, and keep people on a property for as long as possible.

One such place was Pensthorpe Waterfowl Park in Norfolk,[6] a largely agricultural area in eastern England with strong historic links to The Netherlands. The park's primary aim is to manage and encourage public access to a nature reserve that features a variety of habitats: woodland, marsh, and grassland. It also keeps a small number of captive birds in landscaped aviaries. "I had read about Piet's work and was much impressed," said Bill Makins, then the owner and director of the park. "I knew that this site, which is basically a series of water-filled gravel pits, would not be suitable for a classic English garden." After first being contacted in 1997, the park was implemented as a Millennium Project in 2000, and veteran plantsman Roy Lancaster performed the opening ceremony. Piet was asked back to do some replanting in 2008, which was also an opportunity to add some more contemporary touches.

Another opportunity to build a garden as a focal point for a visitor attraction came in 1998, when Sir Charles and Lady Caroline Legard asked Piet to design a garden for them in the walled former kitchen garden of Scampston Hall in North Yorkshire. The couple had moved to the property in 1994 and undertaken the restoration of a rather dilapidated house. With that task complete, attention turned to the garden. "I had read a bit about him" Caroline recalls. "It seemed all the kind of plants he grew were the kind of things that do well here. We have light and dry soil, so his plant palette seemed ideal ... John Coke organized a lecture at Bury Court, so I went to see him ... I asked him afterward about working with us. He was quite cautious at first, but when I told him it would be open to the public, I think that changed his mind."

Practically any country house owned by a person of social standing in the British Isles features a walled garden. Some date back to the eighteenth century, but most to the nineteenth. Few now fulfill their original purpose, so innovative solutions for what to do with the space have been many and varied. Selling them off as building plots has been one solution—in Sussex in 1961, my mother purchased one herself, so being brought up there has probably shaped my thinking ever since! Others make them into a largely decorative garden, and run it as a visitor attraction business; this has proved successful in several places. Scampston also includes a café and teaching facilities, and is aiming at developing a market for educators as well as tourists.

Designing a garden within four walls is, of course, to work within an inescapable framework, so Piet's familiarity with geometric Dutch spaces proved to be an advantage. Caroline says that "when he started on the design, it all came out at once. We only tweaked one thing, and that was because of the measurements. Some designers go back and back over an idea—it's like trying to rework a painting. It is never as good as if it all comes out at one very strong creative moment. I was thrilled, as those things always work best."

The major constraint was financial, which made Caroline determined to propagate as much as she could herself. "Fortunately," she recalls, "we had a very good head gardener, a very good plantsman. He was keen as mustard to propagate everything, so we sat down and worked out that we needed ... five hundred *Astrantia* 'Claret'—we started off with ten—and six thousand *Molinia caerulea*—from an original fifty. It took four years, but we propagated all the herbaceous stuff ourselves." Although the design was largely finalized in 1999, planting

Lobelia x *speciosa* 'Vedrariensis,' a plant that blooms in late summer and early autumn, top, and Pensthorpe Nature Reserve, right and following pages 186–195.

Two views of the walled gardens at Scampston Hall in North Yorkshire.

was staged over a number of years as plants became available from the propagation program. "We got into a routine where Piet came over twice a year, worked all day until late, and stayed overnight." Caroline recalls how impressed she was with the single-minded way Piet worked at the planting. "He was quite silent, it was quite amazing. He just picked up plants and laid them out ... he actually ticked me off a few times because I was trying to be so economical with the plants."

Another story Caroline tells about Piet gives an insight into how he works: "He has an extraordinarily good eye for the smallest detail. He walked into the garden one day and stood at one end of a big path that goes through lots of grasses. It is about a hundred and sixty feet (fifty meters) long, and contains thousands of brick pavers. He said, 'Caroline, it's not straight,' I went really quiet, then I asked the mason who laid it about that, and he told me it was two inches off-center ... there are a pair of lime trees at one end and yew hedges at the other, and he had had to get it centered on both of them. I was flabbergasted. Piet didn't say anything, he just went off and did other things. A few hours later he came back and said he knew what to do ... he suggested we could break the line, lift two courses of bricks and lay them the other way round, and that would solve the problem. It worked."

Walled gardens are rarely exactly square, but as Caroline notes with hers, Piet "managed to make it look symmetrical. At one end, in the summer box border, there are six box cubes and in the spring box border there are seven, but they line up. It's just so clever." While Piet planned the positioning of the structure and the formal elements meticulously, the main area of perennial planting, the "perennial meadow" area he laid out on site, without a diagram.

Scampston has now become a well-known garden to the British gardening public. The fact that its location is in the cool and dry northeast, in a light and rather infertile soil, has made it a particularly important place in helping to educate gardeners. School groups now use the garden and the estate for lessons, and there are plans to launch a heritage and learning center. Its combination of graphic and contemporary formality and richly textured perennials makes it instructive for designers as well as gardeners.

In 1999, *Méér Droomplanten,* Piet's second book with Henk, was published. It refined and added to the range of plants the previous collaboration had set out. This was more or less the palette of plants that also formed the bulk of Piet's designs. It addresses the reader as both gardener and designer—someone who wants to lay out an attractive garden and think about their plants artistically, but who also is aware of needing to think about how much work they will have to do to maintain them. Discussions between the two authors led to a series of categories that makes sense to someone who is looking at plants for both design and long-term care. Henk's considerable knowledge of plant ecology certainly played a major role in the success of that focus.

Looking at the book's structure reveals much about Piet's plant usage. In the introduction, it is made plain that species requiring specialist habitats, such as eternally wet soil or very good drainage, are not considered. Neither are "specialist plants," which are delicate and all too easily smothered by neighbors. The growing of plants via "artificial props and bolstering" such as pesticides, "armies of laborers," and "extra feeding" is frowned upon. The focus is very clearly on resilience and longevity. The book is divided into three sections: Tough, Playful, and Troublesome. "Tough" referred to long-lived and resilient genera like *Cimicifuga* (now *Actaea*), *Geranium*, and *Helianthus* and features subsections on winter silhouettes, giant plants, grasses, and bulbs; "Playful" to those plants that tend to self-seed, which we now know often correlates with being short-lived, as well as a category for biennials; the "Troublesome" section covers shorter-lived perennials like *Echinacea purpurea* and those whose performance is unpredictable, such as the many russet-shaded *Achillea* hybrids. There was also a short section devoted to "Demanding Plants" and another devoted to those described as "Failing the Test." It is not often that garden books include negatives.

Such a focus on adaptable species—what an ecologist might describe as "generalists"—marks a clear innovation in the way of writing reference material. German literature, at least as influenced by the Hansen school, has focused on choosing plants for particular conditions; the British are also interested in manipulating conditions to accommodate favorite plants. The history of perennial gardening has largely been about growing a relatively small number of high-intensity "flower power" plants to a very high standard: peonies, delphiniums, chrysanthemums,

Michelmas daisies. Each genus is dominated by a large, indeed a vast, range of cultivars. Looking through nursery catalogues from earlier in the twentieth century always reveals a good range of "perennials," that is the also-ran A-Z list of mostly unhybridised species. They were very much a minority element, however. In Germany, Karl Foerster's sage advice and a strong commitment to naturalism in gardening ensured that these plants were never forgotten. In The Netherlands and Britain, it almost felt as if these plants had to fight their corner. The two books by Piet and Henk finally brought them out into the open and promoted their virtues—and outlined their important potential as design elements.

Piet and I also had our first book published together in 1999, *Designing with Plants*, with the London-based Conran Octopus. I had suggested to Piet that we do a book together two years previously, to explore his basic design philosophy. I had written about Piet for *The Garden* (the membership magazine of the Royal Horticultural Society) and for the *Financial Times*. A book seemed the obvious next step.

The volume tried to outline Piet's essential design language by looking at the distinct shapes perennials take—or, more precisely, their flower heads and to some extent, foliage. It talks about spires, buttons and globes, plumes, etc. Looking back some sixteen years later, I am slightly surprised to see some spreads based on color too, but then the zeitgeist was so dominated by color (thanks to the Popes at Hadspen House and several successful books on color) that I think we felt we had to think in color terms too. It also featured sections on structure and filler plants, using grasses and umbellifers, architecture—by which we meant clipped woody plants—and a section entitled "Breaking the Rules." This last is something that was fundamental, and indeed still is, to Piet's thinking. Breaking free from traditions in planting design and the formulaic assemblies of predictable plants was at the core of his design work from the very beginning. A major section was also entitled "Moods." We outlined the impact of the more subtle and hard-to-pin-down aspects of planting design, such as the play of light, movement, harmony, control, and "mysticism." I am still not 100 percent sure I know what we meant by this category, apart from a lot of mist in the pictures, but it looked good and sounded good. Finally we ended with the almost compulsory section on seasonal interest: spring without a tulip in sight, and a section

One of Oudolf's favorite maxims is, "a plant is only worth growing if it also looks good when it is dead."

headed "Death," which was quite possibly the first time a garden book had used it as a heading, *without* being negative about it.

My role for this book was very much as a mouthpiece for Piet. As a plant-orientated gardener, occasional designer, and former nurseryman, I think I am someone who Piet feels that he can trust to articulate and explain what he does. I remember going to Hummelo for nearly a week in February 1998. It was very cold, so we hardly ventured out into the garden. Piet and I would sit and work, and every two to three hours or so Anja would pop into Piet's study with bread and cheese, or coffee and cake. I would ask Piet questions of course, and we would pore over plans and photographs. Especially photographs. Piet thinks visually, so my task is to try to articulate his vision. Photographs have always been effective at helping him explain his methodology, particularly since he has photographed his own work so thoroughly.

Piet as Photographer

I noticed very early on how Piet assiduously, continuously, and systematically photographs his work. "It is a way of recording and evaluating what I do," he says. Often, when I have been staying at Hummelo, I will find Piet in the garden soon after dawn, camera in hand. On one early visit, we set off in the morning mist to photograph a client's garden nearby. Photography has in fact been a crucial part of his success as a designer, and has played an important role in helping us change our view of plants and natural beauty.

It took me a while to realize that Piet is actually quite technically minded. Although he still makes hand-drawn plans with colored pencils, he is always on top of the latest releases in cameras, computers, and devices. He was using a digital camera, in fact, well before many professional garden photographers were.

Piet has provided nearly all the photographs of his work for the books we have worked on together. This is unusual for a garden designer, as the profession tends to rely on the work of professional photographers to represent itself. Although photographers are still regular visitors of Hummelo, the images in our books are mostly Piet's, and reflect his own personal vision. It also enables him to document the smallest of changes and in that sense it is a vital part of garden and landscape design.

A key part of Piet's philosophy, and one ultimately derived from Henk Gerritsen's thinking, is to seek beauty in nature where it has not been sought before. Seed heads, yellowing leaves, and emerging spring shoots will grab his attention as much as a colorful flower—in fact, rather more quickly. Photographing this work and publishing it has helped to educate us all in looking at plants and plantings in a different way, and to get far more out of them. He has undoubtedly had an influence on professional garden photographers. Back in the late 1990s, pictures of winter perennials coated in hoarfrost in our first book made quite an impact. Many gardeners at the time still cut their plants down to ground level in late autumn, consigning potential artistic material to the compost heap. The next few years saw many a photographer anxiously scanning the weather forecast for signs of a possible freeze; a flurry of frosty gardens appeared in magazines after that, at least until they—and Piet—got rather bored with that particular angle.

The natural planting movement has, like any movement in art or design, not only presented new ideas to the public, but also taught that public how to see and appreciate its work. Planting in public places and private gardens has traditionally valued human-directed order over the apparent chaos of nature. A bio-diversity agenda, the valuing of plant and invertebrate species disregarded (or even shunned) in the past, has helped many see more naturalistic planting in a positive light. However, most of the public still expects designed plantings to reveal an intentional and deliberate hand. One of the most significant aspects of Piet's work has been to help in this shift, not only in creating plantings that, for many onlookers, appear natural—however much of an artistic conceit this may actually be—but to also make us reinterpret what "natural beauty" means.

The Plant Palette

There is no doubt that Piet's work, alongside that of Henk Gerritsen, has done a great deal to broaden the general appreciation of a perennial's beauty, and has widened our plant palette in the process. His attention to the autumnal aspect of dying perennials and seed heads in particular has been transformative. This should not be mistaken for morbidity; as Piet says, "I discover beauty in things that on first sight are not beautiful. It is a journey in life to find out what real beauty is—and to notice that it is everywhere."

Piet has always worked with a core range of perennials that grow well for him, essentially species that thrive in a continental climate and tend to look at their best from early summer onward. People sometimes wonder why he does not do more with spring flowers (bulbs and shrubs) or woody plants. There is somehow the expectation that a garden designer has to work with everything that can possibly be grown in a particular climate. Would we expect that of an artist? Would I go to a friend who is a highly acclaimed potter, and say "What about sculpture? Don't just do pots, try carving the clay instead." I probably wouldn't. We respect the choice of media artists make, but perhaps expect too much from other design-centered professions. The saying about being a "Jack of all trades and a master of none" holds particularly true for garden designers. Specialism and focus breed virtuosity in a way that versatility does not.

Piet does use trees and shrubs, but very much as part of an overall design that is still focused on perennials. However, since his reputation and the media coverage he has received are now so tied up with perennials, his appreciation of woody plants is always in danger of going unnoticed. Given the opportunity, he loves the chance to do more with them. A good opportunity arrived with the need to create a sheltering scarf of shrubs around a large private garden on Nantucket, and the light woodland he created along parts of the High Line was a golden opportunity to develop a true plant community where the perennial understory is arguably the minor element.

Spring interest for Piet is about the form and texture of plants as they begin to grow—the kind of beauty that can be easily overlooked when it's surrounded with colorful bulbs and flowering shrubs. Most of

Mertensia virginica, Dicentra formosa, Helleborus orientalis and *Uvularia flava*, top, and *Anemone mertensia dicentra* in early spring at Hummelo, below.

us are guilty of failing to notice anything else in that season. And, to be frank, the public expects a certain amount of spring vibrancy. Fortunately, a spring garden of bulbs and other summer-dormant perennials can be more or less superimposed over summer-interest perennials. Increasingly, Piet is adding bulb planting to his projects, but his focus is on small bulbs such as crocus, leucojum, and anemone and spring-flowering summer-dormant plants like *Mertensia virginica* and trillium. Indeed ever since the High Line, Piet has been making bulb plans as a matter of course to accompany his perennial plans.

On some projects, for example in the Lurie Garden in Chicago and at The Battery in New York, he has worked with Jacqueline van der Kloet as bulb designer. She has helpfully had funding from the International Bulb Center. Jacqueline tends to work with a bold and strongly colorful bulb palette that often includes tulips and daffodils. Anyone who looks closely at their work together, however, will see the emerging foliage of epimediums and hostas, and fuzzy clumps of grasses coming back to life. In these projects, the complementary timelines of spring and summer plantings mean that two artists can occupy one space.

For those of us who live on Europe's western fringes or around the Mediterranean and hence experience mild winters, a whole suite of plants is available that are not part of the Northern European Oudolf palette. Many of these are evergreen sub-shrubs or wintergreen perennials, including some with origins in the Southern Hemisphere. Piet will rise to the occasion and work with them when necessary—such as when he designed a small private garden near Barcelona in 1999, or for the gravel garden at Bury Court—but so far they have remained at the fringes. He sometimes uses *Agapanthus*, *Crocosmia*, and *Libertia* if climatic conditions allow.

Shade plants have always been a part of Piet's palette, but since the majority of plantings he has been commissioned to work on are in open conditions, and these are the "default" for planting design, we tend not to see his shade work as much as perhaps we might. Similarly, he can skew his plant palette toward particularly wet or dry conditions—indeed, these present an opportunity for him to use some favorite plants—but many of those plants cannot be used so much in other situations. These include the large-leaved *Darmera* and *Rodgersia*.

A point to be made about plant palettes generally is that if a designer develops a successful palette, they have already done most of the work. As the German and Swiss developers of mixed planting systems have discovered, a visually compatible combination of plants distributed randomly (fifteen to twenty in their case) is very pleasing.[7] A limited plant palette is easy to work with and allows a desired graphic effect to be created with just a few plants, but after a while of course such repetition can become boring. Too much plant diversity in a given space, however, overloads our ability to appreciate the whole. Designers have strong opinions on this question. I remember being with a group that included James van Sweden at a "plantsman's garden" in Portland, Oregon, and noticing mid-visit that he had wandered off. When I found him, he was standing alone in the rain on the other side of the road. "I can't stand this mess," he hissed.

A fundamental reason for Piet's success lies perhaps in his ability to balance coherence and complexity. There is always enough of the same sort of plant to give it instant visual impact, but his plantings include so many different varieties that its complexity engages as well. Complexity is relatively easy to achieve—all it takes are lots of different plants. Coherence, however, is difficult both to achieve and to describe. I would simply suggest that, over the years, Piet has been experimenting with many different ways of achieving coherence.

Despite the wide range of plants in Piet's mature palette, the rough similarity of many of his plants creates a fundamental visual unity. That color is not of major importance to him has the paradoxical effect of removing it from the equation. Color-driven gardeners and designers are perhaps inevitably drawn toward highly bred plants that feature flowers as a high proportion of their biomass. Blocks of color are also more likely to look discordant than smaller ones. Although a great many of the plant varieties in the Oudolf palette are cultivars or hybrids, they all retain the natural flower-to-leaf proportion of their wild ancestors. That all are from a very broadly similar climate zone also helps create unity; those of us from maritime climates where we can mix and match with impunity run the risk of creating plantings with a visual lack of clarity, let alone discipline.

Piet's plant palette has changed remarkably little over time. Certain species seem to dominate during particular phases, but they rarely disappear. Early photographs, for example, seem to include a great deal of the tall, statuesque, and fleshily-pink *Eupatorium maculatum* and mounds of scarlet *Persicaria amplexicaulis*. These are still present, thirty years later, but are less dominant. The main changes to his overall selections have been:

1 Reduction in the use of shorter-lived species, or those that cause a variety of management problems. In the early years, quite a number of biennials appeared in Piet's gardens; he made a strong point about the structural role of umbellifers, for example. These and short-lived perennials that reproduce by seeding are unpredictable—sometimes they will not seed and therefore die out, or they seed so much they become weedlike. A great many perennials are also not truly perennial, but have a lifespan of three years and upward. Consequently, these are used much less now. If a project will have the kind of management capable of replacing plants that may potentially disappear, then Piet will use them; if not, he will forego them. Short-lived self-seeders *can* be introduced he says, but only when the planting is mature and most of the ground is dominated by true perennials. *Verbascum* and *Digitalis* are two examples of superb genera of biennial or short-lived seeders that he once used frequently, but now more rarely.

   It is a sad but true fact that many short-lived plants are very good in terms of structure. *Agastache* are one example, *Echinacea* another, though it is more long-lived in North America than in Europe. Neither genera is necessarily any longer part of the palette for Piet's large-scale plantings where maintenance is likely to be problematic, for the reasons discussed above. Umbellifers including *Angelica*, *Foeniculum*, *Peucedanum*, and *Pimpinella* have also fallen out of his favor, although domestic gardeners should be encouraged to use them. *Selenium* seems more durable, and is still used. *Verbena bonariensis* and *V. hastata* used to appear regularly, but are singularly unpredictable. I distinctly remember a conversation in the late 1990s in which Piet said something to me

Late-summer perennials in bloom at Hummelo.

Two plants Oudolf often uses, *Panicum virgatum* 'Shenandoah,' top, and *Phlox paniculata* 'Dixter,' below.

along the lines of "everyone is using *Verbena bonariensis* now, so I'm going to stop."

Some other plants have been dropped because they seem generally unreliable: the startlingly red grass *Imperata cylindrica* seems very picky about where it grows, while *Helianthus salicifolius*, which has unique tall stems with fine foliage, tends to be too weak to support itself.

2 An increase in grasses since the late 1990s. We have already seen how Piet's knowledge of grasses translated into wider use from the late 1990s onward. North American prairie grasses still have great commercial potential, and as new cultivars appear, they are beginning to feature in a broad range of designs. *Sporobolus heterolepis* is one such species that Piet feels he can use "as-is." In the case of others, it has taken nursery selection work to produce varieties Piet is comfortable employing. An example is *Schizachyrium scoparium,* which can be short-lived and floppy; the High Line includes 'The Blues,' an improved seed strain with good foliage color, bred by Jelitto Seeds, a German company. "It still flops, but nowadays there are new cultivars that don't," Piet points out.

3 An increase in North American genera since working on the Lurie Garden project in the early 2000s, e.g. *Parthenium*, *Pycnanthemum*, *Ruellia*, and *Zizia*. These do not necessarily flourish in Europe, as some appear to need high summer temperatures to establish, although *Pycnanthemum muticum*, *Ruellia*, and *Zizia* species do well. Among familiar genera he often uses unfamiliar species for interest, such as *Euphorbia corollata* and *Eupatorium hyssopifolium*. *Monarda bradburiana* is a recently introduced species, and is often confused with *M. fistulosa*. Its greater persistence and compact habit is leading Piet and other practitioners increasingly to use it instead.

WILDER AND WILDER

Is there a directional arrow to Piet's work? A distinct and overriding tendency that makes all his design innovation fall into a coherent pattern? Stefan Mattson would argue that "his style is becoming wilder and wilder." I agree. Piet has a clear design trajectory. He has grown out from under the shadow of the immense and magnificent tree that was the Mien Ruys, Bauhaus-originated style to develop planting techniques that can best be described as a kind of re-created nature. As the twentieth century turned into the twenty-first, his new projects began to show a growing sophistication in how plants were put together. In particular, Piet's work began to show a shift from block planting to "intermingling."

Leo den Dulk, whose passion for garden history gives him the long perspective, says "Piet is in the Dutch tradition, as we have naturalists who become gardeners ... Thijsse and his group were gardeners and naturalists. The big names in gardening were also very interested in nature. Mien Ruys, for example, was also interested in wild plants even though she did not necessarily include them in her schemes. And many gardens were influenced by ideas from the naturalists."

This trajectory from the architecturally ordered to the almost-wild can be summarized in broad stages:

- a gradual abandonment of clipped shrubs,
- a movement from block planting toward intermingling,
- a movement from one method of arranging perennials to a multiplicity of methods, i.e. as part of a growing complexity,
- a greater 'naturalism,' i.e. the *appearance* of being natural plant communities, or at least natural plant communities that we humans find aesthetically pleasing,
- a clear focus on maximizing the proportion of plant varieties that are long-lived in most planting situations.

In looking at Piet's planting over time, we can recognize a trend toward growing complexity. Stefan Mattson, in the unique position of having commissioned Piet four times, may be the person best situated to have witnessed his design evolve. Regarding Enköping's Dreampark, he says "in the block planting he did, the plants fit together in a good way with their neighbors. When I first saw it, it seemed strange. Every area was the same size, about three meters, but it worked very well. The way he works now takes more plant knowledge. At Skärholmen we have the different planting mixtures, and we have narrow paths for maintenance staff that go between and separate them, making the borders clearer, which makes it easier for staff to know what is meant to be there."

The Dreampark in Enköping, Sweden.

Reflecting on the block planting style of Dreampark, Stefan says that "at a conference in 2013, Piet was asked if he would do it differently today, but he avoided answering that question ... in fact, I liked the way he did the Dreampark. I would not change anything. The block planting worked, and I don't think you can throw that style away."

More plant knowledge *is* needed to maintain more complex plantings. More skill is needed in designing them too. Those who are designing or commissioning for situations where there is only a limited maintenance staff or budget available would do well to consider this. Reducing the number of species or the complexity of the planting simply does make maintenance easier. The earlier phases of Piet's career are perhaps more appropriate for study for those who cannot guarantee high levels of skilled management.

Accolades in England

The Chelsea Flower Show has long been considered the world's leading such event. Traditionally it was intended to provide a showpiece for nurseries and others in the business to promote their products, most of which would be put on display in the great central marquee (no one "in the know" would ever call it a tent). For most of its history it lasted only three days, but it has long been both a vital horticultural event and a date on the social calender of British high society.

There have always been show gardens around the perimeter of the site, historically constructed by garden design-and-build companies or nurseries who offered similar services. During the 1990s, as the emphasis of the show began to change, nurseries were increasingly reluctant to show in the marquee. This development coincided with an enormous increase in the popularity of garden design; increasing incomes brought many more people into the market for having their gardens professionally laid out. The design revolution was greatly stimulated (although some might say artificially inflated) by the attention of sensationalized television shows that recorded dramatic weekend transformations of gardens, alongside a great deal of hype from celebrity presenters. Show gardens increasingly became the focus at Chelsea, with leading designers vying for publicity. Television and newspaper coverage built the show into a major media spectacle.

Gardens Illustrated magazine had sponsored a show garden at Chelsea in 1997, designed by Christopher Bradley-Hole, the first of many the London-based designer has made for the event. "It helped launch him into a new career," recalled Rosie Atkins. "And he got besotted with Piet and fascinated by Rob Leopold." Christopher is an interesting example of a designer who has skirted the edge of the perennials movement; he has long been interested by planting and is very inventive, but he also holds very much to a distinctly graphic and architectural style. He was friends with John Coke who, in 2003, commissioned him to create a new front garden at Bury Court.

Rosie remembers in 1997 that "Arne Maynard marched into the office at *Gardens Illustrated*, desperate to get connected. He was very much a starry-eyed newcomer … he was saying he would like to work with

Eryngium giganteum self-seeding in Oudolf's border at Wisley, the Royal Horticultural Society's flagship garden in Surrey, England.

Piet." Rosie suggested that he collaborate with Piet on a Chelsea Garden together for the magazine for the year 2000. "It was an interesting combination. I don't think it had ever happened before at Chelsea, two designers working together," she says. "It wasn't easy, and neither of them had ever done it before. I ended up being a project manager. It could have turned out like a complete dog's dinner but in the end it turned out well—got a gold and the Best in Show award. Piet remembers how "Rosie asked me to do the garden with Arnie. I could not do on it my own ... the cloud hedging was his idea, but the wall, painting, and fountain—that all came out of collaboration." For Piet it was "a one-off event. You have to live [near London], and if you don't have staff, it is very complicated to do Chelsea."

The garden, dubbed "Evolution," included a red wall backing a painting that was flanked by a cloud-pruned tree. In front of this, squares of clipped box surrounded circular concrete water features. To the sides, Piet's planting took over. It featured red *Astrantia major* varieties, *Cirsium rivulare* 'Atropurpureum,' and the dark bronze-purple leaves of *Actaea simplex* 'Atropurpurea'—all picked up the color of the wall.

Designing a garden for the Royal Horticultural Society's garden at Wisley, in Surrey, was another sign that Piet had "arrived" in Britain. A residual chauvinistic tendency survived in Britain through at least the first few years of the first decade of the twenty-first century—it was often made clear that non-British architects and others were distinctly not welcome to design major public projects. It was a breakthrough to see the RHS reaching out to Piet for innovation.

Penelope Hobhouse, then at the height of her reputation as a garden designer, lobbied behind the scenes for Piet to be given the job of creating a new double border. The area was intended as the first stage of a major new development launched by the RHS. The concept was to create a parallel to the old double borders that lead from the entrance of the garden to the base of Battleston Hill. These borders, laid out in the early twentieth century were, by the late nineties, a clear anachronism; they were valid only as an example of how rigid old-style perennial planting was (they have since been modernized). The RHS wanted a contemporary version to lead down to what was to be the site of a new glasshouse. The borders would be visible not just by people walking down the middle but also from a "mount," a hillock planted with native wildflowers and dwarf apple trees at the upper end of the borders.

Although the finished borders are stunning, especially in late autumn when the grasses are at their best, the maintenance and management staff have made some alterations that have caused them to begin to drift from the original plan. Piet notes that, "it is not the original design any more."

BLENDING AND INTERMINGLING

Many of Piet's larger projects through the 2000s involved block planting and scattering. At the beginning of this period, however, he had begun to experiment with a qualitatively different approach: creating plant blends where several varieties are mixed together. The result is more naturalistic and more complex, but it offers considerable opportunity to increase seasonal interest in a given space. In working with blending, he was not alone. German practitioners, with their very strong tradition of an ecological basis for planting design, had been working with it for some time. Others in the U.S.—and in Britain—had been working with it too, but only on a small scale. "Intermingling" as this device has become known, is discussed in depth in our book *Planting, a New Perspective*, with the understanding that this is a complex approach that we have only just begun to explore. We openly acknowledge that we have much to learn about it yet.

Piet turned to blending plants because it hugely increases the range of possibilities of creating attractive and indeed functional combinations, and because it introduces a more naturalistic note. Early blends tended to be very simple, often combining just two plants. A very good example is the combination of *Molinia caerulea* with *Calamintha nepeta* ssp. *nepeta*. The grass has a very upright habit and tends to leave gaps between its clumps, whereas the calamintha has a distinct central growth point with foliage that sprawls outward (i.e. the plant itself does not spread). The two forms together complement each other by filling space

Plants arranged in "drifts" at the Lurie Garden in Chicago.

Autumn at Potters Fields Park along the banks of the Thames in London.

effectively. Another combination sought to overcome the rather awkward upright growth of perovskia varieties in cultivation by planting *Origanum* or *Geranium* species between them.

From these very simple beginnings, Piet's intermingling has grown ever more complex. As any mathematician will tell you, the range of possibilities will grow exponentially the more variables you consider. For a planting designer, it is exciting territory. From around 2010, Piet's work began increasingly to feature intermingling, often juxtaposed with block planting or with matrix planting.

The Wisley garden (2001) was one of the first examples where Piet used intermingling on a large scale; it was composed almost entirely of bands, each of which was a blend of around five or six varieties. Potters Fields Park on the banks of the Thames in London (2007) used a similar approach but stretched the bands out to create long drifts with straight edges and angular bends. Like Gertrude Jekyll's drifts, these gave a very different impression when seen head-on as opposed to end-on. Berne Park (2010) exploited the circular labyrinth-like nature of the site to create a series of blends that can be appreciated as one walks around the path and toward the garden's center. Skärholmen Park (2010) adopts a very roughly similar approach of using concentric circles, but in a more conventional urban park space. In both cases, scatter plants serve to link different blends and areas.

MINI
564

CROSSING THE ATLANTIC

Chicago's Lurie Garden: The First North American Project

By the 1990s the Oehme van Sweden practice in Washington D.C. was clearly setting the pace in terms of planting design on the East Coast. In the Midwest however, garden and landscape design had become stuck in a sterile model of trees/shrubs/mown grass. Chicago was slowly emerging from what had been a couple of decades of decline for major American cities in the formerly industrial "Rust Belt," and it was faced with plenty of areas urban dereliction awaiting redevelopment.

A particular eyesore was adjacent to the center of downtown—as city mayor Richard M. Daley himself noted one day as he looked out of the window of his dentist's office on Michigan Avenue. He began a campaign to clean up this messy patch of abandoned former railway land not far from the shores of Lake Michigan. With his prompting, a proposal was launched for building a new park on top of an underground parking garage on the site, which would itself be built over the tracks of the Metra/Illinois Central Railroad. It was to become known as Millennium Park. The Ann and Robert Lurie Foundation provided funding for the garden, with the understanding that the eventual design was to be chosen by competition.

The year 2000 saw Piet enter his proposal for this new public garden. In fact, he joined forces with Gustafson Guthrie Nichol (GGN). Once of its principals, Kathryn Gustafson, had already achieved a reputation as one of the world's leading landscape architects. She "thought his work was extraordinary ... our work was so different, it was complementary."

When the announcement came that GGN was the winning entrant in October 2000, Piet realized he had a major project on his hands. It would not only be his first in North America, he would also be working with a famously headstrong colleague. The result, however, has been a spectacular success, due in large part to a mutual respect between landscape architect and plantsman. Gustafson thinks that "Piet has changed the way landscape architects see gardeners and horticulture professionals. They see them with a better understanding of what they can bring to a project ... we had decided that we didn't know his type of perennial planting well enough, and we needed to bring in expertise."

Every day, hundreds to thousands of people walk through Chicago's Lurie Garden. Many stop to admire the plants: bulbs and flowering trees in spring, perennials through the summer months, and masses of grass and wildflower seed heads in autumn. Even in winter there are plants to see. Instead of crushing them, the fine dry snow of the Midwest tends to gather on and around seed heads, highlighting their silhouettes with its whiteness—at least until they are completely buried. They are cut down by maintenance staff at the end of the winter, and left as mulch.

The Lurie Garden has been an eye-opener for many Chicagoans. It shows that it is possible to grow a wide range of perennials in a place not renowned for a temperate climate; it also illustrates how many regionally native plants have garden potential. The city's Latin motto *Urbs in horto* may translate as "city in a garden," and the city may have many fine parks, but the idea of growing a perennial-based public space in the middle of the city was a near-revolutionary one. At the end of the twentieth century, garden-making was not a pastime that figured highly in the culture of the American Midwest. The area did have some history of local design, however: Wilhelm Miller had promoted prairie vegetation for gardens and landscapes in the early part of the twentieth century, at about the same time that Frank Lloyd Wright was leading the Prairie School of architecture; as later did Jens Jensen.

Prairie restoration and the use of prairie plants in landscapes, however, had been a quiet-but-growing movement for some time, particularly since the start of the restoration in 1962 of an area of prairie at the Morton Arboretum outside Chicago (it is now known as the Schulenberg Prairie). That effort was largely limited to ecologists and those who took a distinctly purist approach to planting; indeed the very notion of "gardening" was largely alien to those who promoted the use of prairie wildflowers as an alternative to lawns and other areas of mown grass. Roy Diblik, however, had made a connection between the native plant movement, domestic gardens, user-friendly landscapes, and he was to become a key part of the Lurie Garden story.

Roy's career started in outdoor education, then moved to parks maintenance. He had also run a native plant nursery, and in 1979 had pioneered the growing of natives in containers, although there was initially very little retail interest. "They were the kind of plants people saw by the side of the road," he recalls. Most of his clients were habitat restorationists, until "perennials began to catch on. It was the Oehme van Sweden work on the East Coast that changed things. I began to sell more echinacea and rudbeckia, and by the early 1980s we were selling hundreds of thousands of plants." In 1991 he got together with two colleagues to start Northwind Perennial Farm, which includes a wholesale nursery, a retail site, and a garden construction and maintenance company. His approach to planting design is closely linked to an acute awareness of the importance of maintenance, and some of the work he has done on planting formulas has parallels with developments in Europe.

By the time Kathryn Gustafson met with Piet, she had already worked out a basic concept for the garden, which was to include theater lighting by designer Robert Israel. Piet's planting had to fit a division made in the garden between an open area (the Light Plate) and an area with more tree planting (the Dark Plate). The Dark Plate needed species that would tolerate increasing shade over time, whereas the Light Plate was more exposed. To the south, architect Renzo Piano was also designing an extension to the Art Institute of Chicago, and Gustafson describes how "we tilted the garden toward the Institute so that a big hedge (dubbed The Shoulder Hedge) at the back the garden became very theatrical. We set the stage for Piet to work in."

Kathryn describes Piet's design: "He started with something quite rigid, and he loosened up over time. It got more contextual as he got to know Chicago. I think Roy Diblik was instrumental in all of this." Diblik remembers that in "July 2001, I got a fax about Piet coming over.

He came with John Coke. It was at about the time of 9/11. I remember how he rolled out a copy of a plan for the Lurie Garden on a workbench. I could see immediately that there had never been anything like this before in the Midwest. We went through the plants, what would work and not work. He got me involved in producing the plants—28,000 plants, with no substitutes. We subcontracted the growing of the easier plants and I did the more difficult ones myself."

The main area of the Lurie Garden, the Light Plate, is open and sunlit. It is situated far enough away from the steel and glass of the buildings of central Chicago that they form a scenic backdrop to the garden instead of looming over it. The ground of the garden has a gentle roll to it, much like the landscape of the Midwest, and Piet's planting enhances these contours. While an ecologist might say that Piet's garden is a stylized representation of a natural prairie, for the city dweller it presents an escape into a large expanse of nature that is nevertheless familiar. The fact that many of the plant species used are prairie natives reinforces this, as do the butterflies that come to feed on the flowers and the wild birds that come for the perennial seed heads.

The Lurie Garden is also significant in planting design history for several other reasons. It is in effect, a roof garden, so its soil depth hovers between 1.5 and 4 feet (0.45 and 1.2 meters). This layer tops a concrete slab that functions as the roof of the parking garage below—one of a growing number of examples of completely artificial, large-scale gardens in urban areas. The complexity of the planting scheme here also shows how far landscape design has come; by comparison, we have the garden at the Art Institute designed by renowned landscape architect Dan Kiley in 1965, which lies just a few hundred meters away. The earlier garden looks quite rigid and tame by comparison.

The popularity of the Salvia River at the Dreampark in Enköping, Sweden, led Piet to attempt something similar here. Its wave shape and flowers in a range of violet-blues in early summer, before much of the Light Plate is in flower, makes an electric impact. "I don't usually repeat things," he says, "but on this occasion I did." In terms of public appeal, it was probably the right thing to do.

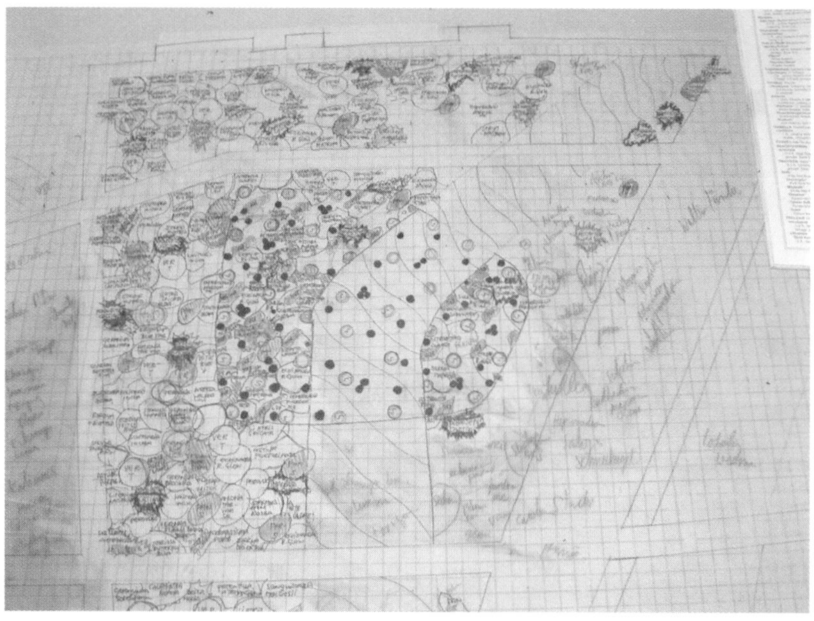

The Lurie Garden in Chicago in development, above and overleaf,
and a planting plan for the space, below.

WELCOME
PLEASE
STAY

SCATTER PLANTS

Piet started to develop an approach to using scatter plants in the late 1990s, and since then has included them in most of his projects. When he returned to Pensthorpe in 2008, to revamp the garden, he added scatter plants such as *Helenium* 'Rubinzwerg,' *Solidago* 'Golden Rain,' *Inula* 'Sonnenstrahl,' and *Molinia caerulea* ssp. *arundinacea* 'Transparent.' He started using this technique for the first time in Trentham.

Essentially, scatter plants are individuals or very small groupings of plants interspersed among blocks of plant varieties or through a matrix planting, breaking up the regularity of the pattern; their distribution is generally quasi-random. They may serve several quite different functions:

- They may link one part of a planting with another, perhaps even creating a strong sense of unity across the whole. At the Giardino delle Vergini in Venice, for example, a number of species were more or less evenly distributed across the entire area.
- They may help to define an area visually, setting it apart from the rest.
- They may break up the chunkiness of blocks. At Trentham, *Baptisia australis* and a few others are used on a small scale, adding a note of surprise.
- They may provide an unexpected focal point in areas otherwise dominated by matrix planting. Scatter plants play an important part on the High Line, particularly in providing interest in the grass matrix in the grassland stretch. A very wide range is used.
- Scatter plants often provide a contrasting note, a splash of color, or a distinct structure that is noticeable at flowering time and sometimes after. *Helenium* 'Rubinzwerg' often appears in this role because its scarlet button flowers on 2-to-2.5-foot-high stems (80 to 140 centimeters), making it a center of attention.
- Scatter plants can also be used to provide interest at a time of year outside the season when a planting is designed to provide its main bloom time, notably spring or autumn.
- They may also provide a long season of structural interest, with *Veronicastrum virginicum* for example.
- They may be used to inject striking color and form for a short period of time, and then quickly become dormant. *Papaver orientale* varieties were used in Bad Driburg (2008) and the Lurie Garden to create this effect. Bulbs can also be used in this way.

Echinacea purpurea used as a scatter plant on the High Line in New York.

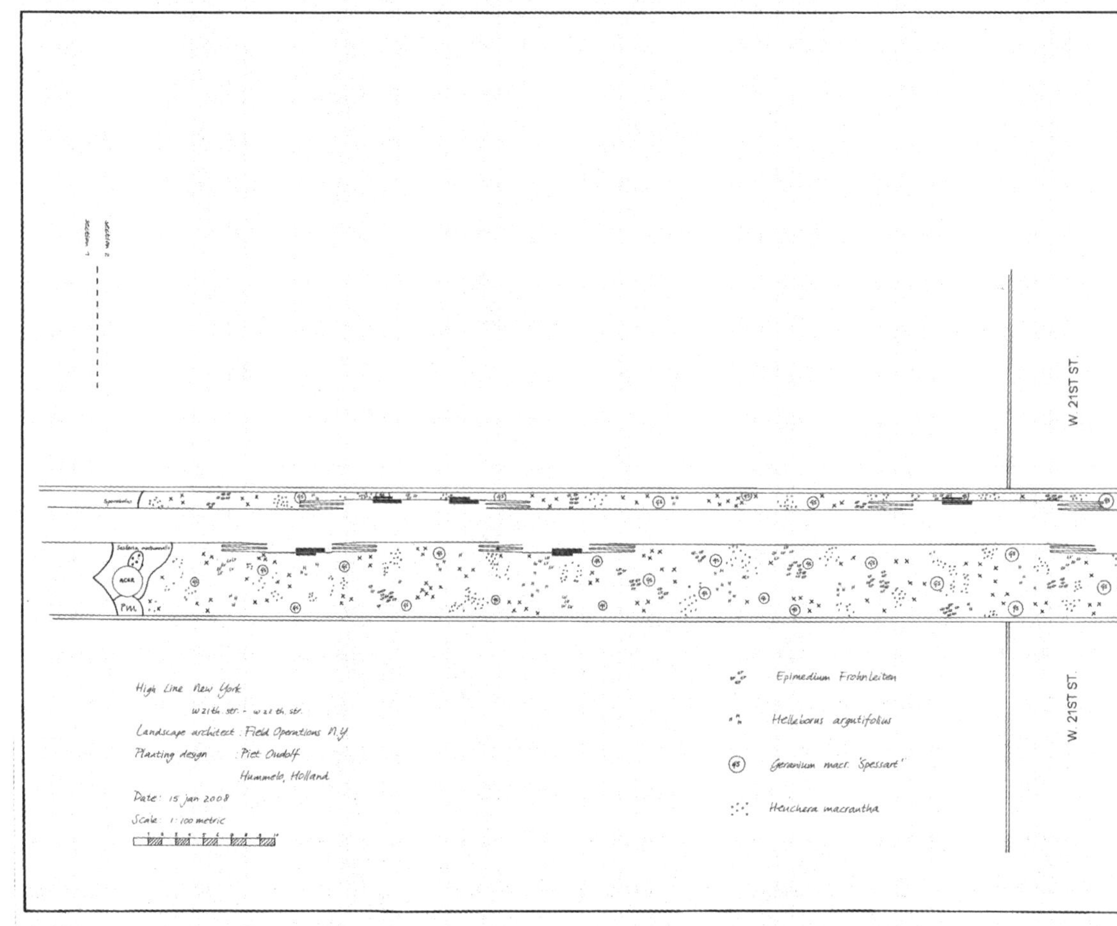

A section of the plan for the High Line showing scatter plant distribution.

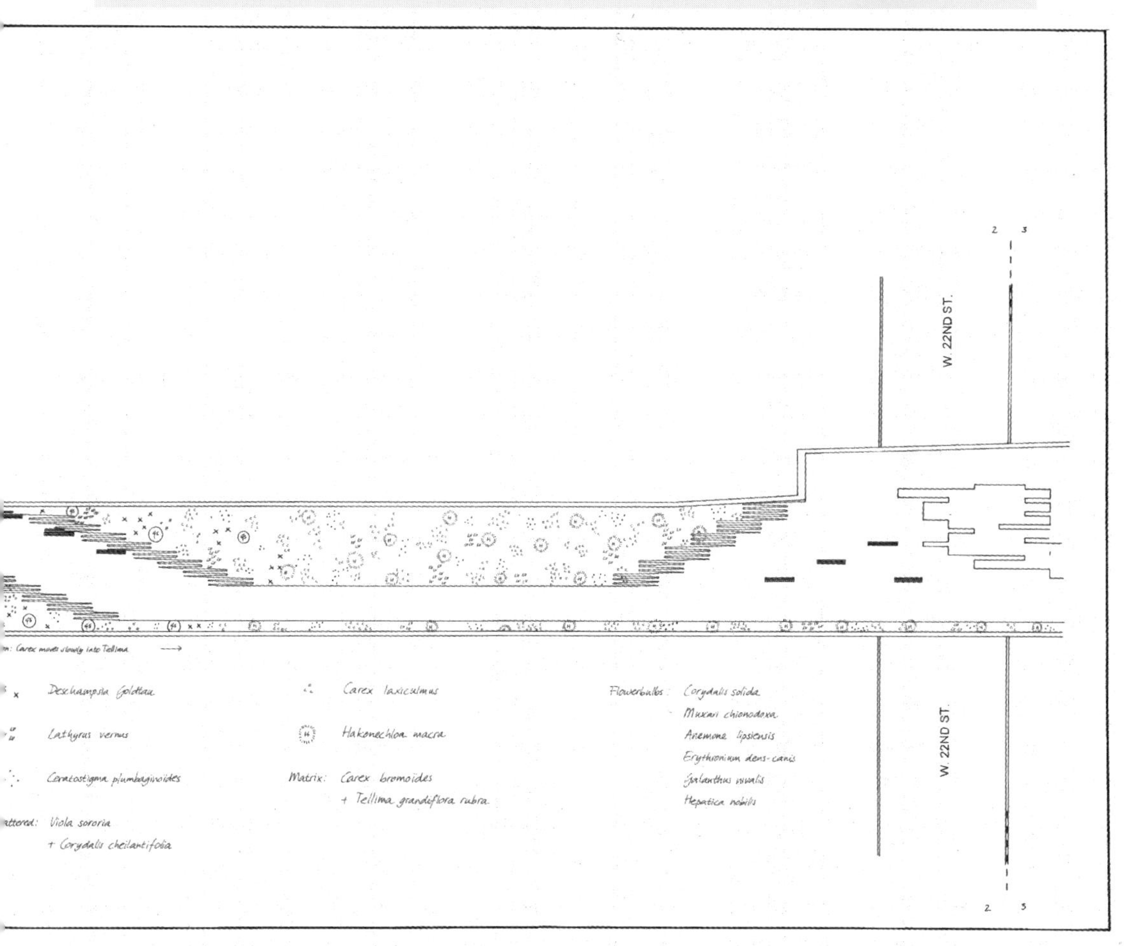

2 3
W. 22ND ST.
n: Carex moves slowly into Tellima →
Deschampsia Goldtau
Lathyrus vernus
Ceratostigma plumbaginoides
attered: Viola sororia
+ Corydalis cheilantifolia
Carex laxiculmus
Hakonechloa macra
Matrix: Carex bromoides
+ Tellima grandiflora rubra
Flowerbulbs: Corydalis solida
Muscari chionodoxa
Anemone lipsiensis
Erythronium dens-canis
Galanthus nivalis
Hepatica nobilis
W. 22ND ST.
2 3

Working with North American Plants

The Lurie Garden provided Piet with his introduction to North American prairie flora. He, and anyone else working with perennials, of course knows that so many of the plants used in Europe are in fact North American in origin. However, since the introduction of these plants (including many species of *Aster*, *Echinacea*, *Helianthus*, and *Solidago*) over a century ago, gardeners using them had little awareness of where they grew in the wild, or that those available in cultivation may only represent a small fraction of the diverse forms in existence in nature. Roy Diblik recalls taking Piet on some early visits to prairie habitats: "In 2002 I took Piet to the Schulenberg Prairie. He was so taken with it. It was a very emotional moment for him. Seeing all the *Baptisia leucantha* in flower made a very powerful impression on him. After that, he changed a lot of the planting in the Lurie plan to include more natives, such as baptisias and eryngiums. He came again in the fall with Anja, and we visited the Markham Prairie south of Chicago. Masses of liatris were in flower."

From that point on, an increasing number of North American plants began to appear in Piet's designs. Other designers and gardeners in Europe began a similar discovery on roughly the same schedule, or perhaps we should say rediscovery, as there had been a similar interest in these plants in the early twentieth century. Many species, and indeed entire genera such as *Baptisia* and *Sporobolus,* which had once been commercially available but had never become popular and so largely disappeared from the nursery trade after World War II were now being grown again and actively promoted by nurseries. The beginnings of an interest in prairie plantings as a low-maintenance, wildlife-friendly style for urban areas started around this time, particularly in England and in Germany. Crucially, North Americans also began to rediscover the beauty and value of their own flora. The Lurie Garden was both a stimulus for this movement as well as a reflection of it. "It really shook up Chicago," says Roy. "When it first went in, a lot of landscape architects in particular were not very receptive. They didn't know how to deal with it, but now everyone loves it and a lot of people name it as the most beautiful spot in the city."

Sorghastrum nutans, top, and *Aster* 'Herfstweelde,' two North American plants that have appeared in Oudolf's designs.

MAINTENANCE FROM A DISTANCE

The Lurie Garden's first chief horticulturalist was Colleen Lockovitch, who remembers that, "I met Piet for the first time in 2005, a few months after I started. He was [in Chicago] on his first evaluation of the garden ... I was nervous, although we had emailed before ... the Lurie Garden had budgeted to have him over every two years to do an evaluation." This, of course, is a rare luxury for a public garden. Jennifer Davit, who took over from Colleen in March 2010, has a close working relationship with Piet, since the level of contact between them is substantially higher than is normal for most projects, public or private. What results is the constant evolution of the Lurie Garden, but under the supervision of its designer.

"We communicate every month by email; we Skype regularly too," says Jennifer, "I'll send him the plan of the garden and I'll put little notes on it to say, this plant isn't working or we want to change it, or it only looks good for two weeks, things like that. He'll put on his own notes on it and send it back to me ... sometimes I send photos too." On the occasions Piet visits, she describes how they look over together "areas of concern, like where the design intent is fading a little, or the plants are moving out of bounds. I like to send photos in advance, perhaps through the season ... I have divided the garden up into beds, to make it easier to reference what we need to do ... he'll make suggestions, and I'll take notes furiously."

Jennifer is proactive in making suggestions for new plants as necessary to replace those that are not thriving. The U.S. plant palette is changing rapidly as nurseries seek out good—and tough—new cultivars from the nation's immensely rich native stock. For example, she recalls finding "*Vernonia* 'Iron Butterfly,' a suggestion made by staff member Laura Young. We loved it, so I suggested using it as a replacement for *Eupatorium* 'Chocolate,' which is seeding everywhere. It flowers at about the same height and time. Piet approved our choice, but other times he might reject something as too commonplace." "Roy [Diblik] also suggests plants we could try," she says. "Like *Solidago* 'Wichita Mountains.' It's upright and blooms late, and its very drought tolerant."

Jennifer is well aware that garden conditions change over time, and that part of her work with Piet involves exploiting the opportunities this offers. "The original design intent has been kept, but the garden is evolving and changing from the original plan," she notes. "A number of the plants that we are now finding successful would not have succeeded at the beginning. Everything was irrigated at first, and some plants did not survive, e.g., *Agastache rupestris* and *Anaphalis* species, things that

Jennifer Davit, director and head horticulturalist of the Lurie Garden, with her team.

seem sensitive to too much water. We realize now that those plants can work if the irrigation is tailored to them. That opens up a whole new palette of plants we can try. It's fun."

As the garden grows, plants of course seed, which is sometimes problematic. Some species have had to be removed, others rigorously dead-headed, but this also offers opportunities for improvement. This has been true for *Gentiana andrewsii*. As Jennifer describes it, "the bottle gentian is a gorgeous plant but it needs the support of other plants—it flops badly. It was originally planted in masses by itself. It survived, but aesthetically it didn't work. We are fortunate as now it is seeding in, and we are transplanting the seedlings so they can get support."

The Boon Garden, top, and Oudolf's exhibition at the 2002 Floriade in The Netherlands, below.

Restrictions Suggest Creative Solutions

Designers tend to take on bigger and bigger jobs as their career advances. If these happen to be for public projects, of course it allows their work to be appreciated by more and more people. The downside is that large projects do not yield the same opportunities for experimentation with ideas that may have worked well in domestic gardens or with smaller plant palettes. One medium-sized garden Piet designed during the time he was working on the Lurie Garden gave him the chance to see what he could do with a restricted site; this was a home garden for the architect Piet Boon. "He gave me complete freedom," Piet says, "but I wanted the design to follow his style of architecture, which is very strong, very personal. It's bold and modern, but its Dutch roots are clearly visible." The site was on the edge of open countryside. The use of perennials and a large, central, formal block of the grass *Sporobolus* around a rectangular pool helped fit the garden into its surroundings. The Boon family went on to commission Piet to make gardens for a number of houses he later designed as well.

Another smaller but gemlike planting to emerge at roughly the same time was a therapeutic garden for the Reumaverpleeghuis (a care center) in Rotterdam in 2002. Piet designed a restful environment with a profusion of seating opportunities. At its core was the concept of easy maintenance coupled with strong design. That same year brought the once-a-decade Floriade, held in Haarlemmermeer. Piet worked with Hein Koningen and Jacqueline van der Kloet (under the overall direction of landscape architect Niek Roozen) on a master plan for key areas around exhibition sites: the entrance, lakeside areas, and a ground layer for areas of woodland. The brief indicated that it was to show how perennials, alongside other plants, could look good over a long season with minimal maintenance. Piet made two borders, one for the sun and other for light shade—these came to play a part in Piet getting his Battery Park commission in New York.

On a much larger scale is the garden Piet made in 2002 for a Luxembourg bank's conference center, which was housed in an old farmhouse on a former farm. It features a wide and expansive, lush and arcadian view. Development of a garden there was already well under way when Piet was commissioned —British couple Paul and Pauline McBride had been employed as its gardeners since 1998. Their focus had been on planting borders and bands of curtain-like hedging. Piet was brought in to create a planting that would transition from the garden to the landscape beyond. A border on a monumental scale proved to be the answer. In its final incarnation it is 165 yards (150 meters) long, and an average of about 30 feet (10 meters) wide, for a total of half a hectare. The sheer scale of the border raises eyebrows at the prospect of maintenance—particularly weeding. Piet's careful design, however, ensures that "this type of planting only takes thirty-five percent of the work of a conventional garden ... if mulched with pine bark, even less." The McBrides agreed, and on returning to Britain several years later, they created an even larger series of borders as a garden they now run as a business, Sussex Prairies.

Twenty Years of Progress

In 2002, the nursery at Hummelo saw its twentieth anniversary. Several neighboring families, which in the countryside means about half a dozen, followed local custom for a wedding or other special event and decorated the entrance to its drive the night before. Piet was now well and truly established as a designer, as well as a resident of Hummelo. Most people who had achieved a similar amount of success would likely be running an office by then, probably with a studio in the nearest big town.

Piet, however, has never chosen to build up a professional staff. He chooses instead to work together with landscape architects for specific projects. "Sometimes I have been tempted to employ people, but in the city it is much easier to get talented people for a long period. Most young people have busy social lives, and you simply cannot offer that here in Hummelo ... I had a fear of taking on the wrong person, and I'm not the sort of person who wants to take on someone and then fire them," he admits.

The absence of an office also points back to Rosie Atkins's analysis of Piet as an artist first and a designer second. Peter Paul Rubens famously had assistants paint for him, and many modern sculptors employ others to build, carve, or weld for them—but in reality most artists do not, cannot, or will not. Creation is an individual thing that cannot be outsourced. Piet is very happy to collaborate and work alongside other people responsible for different aspects of a project, and he will occasionally employ people to calculate the number of plants needed, to source them, to evaluate project conditions, and to help set out plants on site—but he cannot delegate the design process any more than a composer could delegate composition. Rosie notes that, "he does not have teams of people. It's a unique way of working. He does work well in a particular kind of collaboration, but he does not want to run a team. He does not want to be responsible for them. He has never wanted to run a design studio." Rosie says that she has been part of conversations between Piet and other designers who look "somewhat wistful" when they discover he is free of the obligations of running a firm.

Planting design is a highly specific skill, and is very different to designing with inanimate materials. Part of Piet's success in larger public projects relies on his willingness to work as part of a team—indeed, he had to learn to rely on others after 2000, when commissions became increasingly complex. More than ever, this is in fact how design professionals and those involved in providing the technical backup to creative projects must work. "I like to work with the architect—it is very cooperative," he says. "My work is still my work, but it happens more and more alongside other people's work. For example, landscape architects design the infrastructure and hardscaping—what they do is part of what I do, and what I do is part of what they do."

For projects in The Netherlands, Piet says, "I have a group of landscape architects I like to work with here. I can ask them to join me, we work on the master plan, and they do the technical aspects. I try to do the planting plan as late as possible to allow for changes, as reality always differs from what was first conceived. But if you are working with a team, like with Field Operations on the High Line, they want your concept before they have even finished their own design, so you have to make changes three or four times and you have to really redo many things, even though they might be based on the initial idea."

Piet usually has around twenty jobs in different stages in progress at any one time, of which about half will be on hold. Some jobs, including almost all public commissions, of course take years from the initial concept to reach completion—some as long as five or even ten. He estimates that he now completes about eight designs a year. Like

Four views of a private garden in West Cork, Ireland, above and right.

anyone in a successful design business, he has also had to learn how to turn projects away, but Piet has always been cautious about taking on commissions. Rosie Atkins remembers one incident when "some woman said to him, 'Come and do my garden. Come for the weekend. Bring your family.' She kept pestering him, so eventually he said 'I have to tell you I have enough friends thank you.'"

Tom de Witte is one younger colleague Piet has employed on a number of occasions, and has indeed passed work on to. Even as a teenager, he was a keen gardener. "I have been familiar with planting plans since I was twelve," he says. "I first heard about Piet Oudolf when I was seventeen, and a couple of months after I got my driver's licence, I borrowed my mum's car and drove over to Hummelo. It was a three-hour drive, so it was quite a journey for me." He studied at Boskoop, a major center for both the nursery trade and for horticulture and design, and then went into landscape design as a career in Belgium. "From 2000," he recalls, "Piet asked me to assist him with projects such as the West Cork garden in Ireland. We went over together to see whether the site was ready for planting. I felt very privileged. I was making plant lists, and for some jobs I would help set the plants when they arrived on site or contact contractors, etc." He is one of the few who has been privy to Piet's design process. "His style is intuitive. He is almost impossible to follow. Standing there, I felt like a wizard's pupil … it is almost impossible to see what is in his head, because as soon as you think you understand something he comes up with something new. A lot of it is experimental. His plantings are so multilayered, but without being overdone."

At the time of publication, Piet's current projects include a number of private gardens, mostly in or near New York, and two projects in Britain that will be publicly accessible. One is with art dealer Hauser & Wirth, who is making a gallery in a complex of old farm buildings near Bruton, Somerset, in southwest England. Part of the plans include a 1.5-acre (6,000-square-meter) garden that will be surrounded by trees and therefore stand as a self-contained garden space. The second will be a "ribbon" of planting several hundred meters long for Queen Elizabeth Park, the successor to Olympic Park created in 2012. There, Piet's work will be near some of the planting created for the Olympics by Nigel Dunnett and James Hitchmough, two professors from the University of

Plans and realization of the Queen Elizabeth Olympic Park in London, above, right, and overleaf.

Spreading Ideas

Gardeners tend to be a generous bunch. A visit to a gardening friend or colleague often involves a spade being produced and driven into the ground to divide a perennial, or some seed being shaken out of a container into an envelope to take away. True gardeners exchange plants and ideas readily. Piet falls very much in this vein. Joyce Huisman remembers how, "lots of English nurserymen would come over to Hummelo and would leave with lots of Piet's plants for free—it is in the characters of Piet and Anja to live generously."

Piet takes things a step further, however, and also extends his generosity to his plans. Many garden and landscape professionals are almost astounded with the freedom with which he gives them away. Almost the first time I met him, I came away with a folder full myself. The secret of course is that he views each plan as a snapshot in time, and he does not repeat himself, so he would never reuse them again. As Warrie Price of The Battery records, "we did a guidebook to the garden and Piet gave me some of his plans to include. I asked him whether he was sure it would be ok to reproduce them. I pointed out people might just go and copy them. His response was, 'I like to give them away. I always have new ideas'."

Like many in his profession, Piet lectures frequently and also disseminates his ideas in that way. As a good photographer, his events are a feast for the eyes as much as an explanation. He has also taught landscape architecture courses at Harvard's Graduate School of Design and run workshops at a number of other places in the U.S., Britain, Austria, and once, in Moscow. Together we have run a number of workshops at Hummelo. He was appointed a visiting professorship at Sheffield's Department of Landscape in 2012, so he also regularly runs classes there.

Piet Oudolf and Noel Kingsbury
Planting Design | Gardens in Time and Space
TIMBER PRESS
DROOMPLANTEN
terra
PIET OUDOLF & NOEL KINGSBURY
PLANTATIONS : NOUVELLES PERSPECTIVES
Méér Droomplanten
Henk Gerritsen en Piet Oudolf
TERRA lannoo
designing with plants
piet oudolf
Piet Oudolf
Landscapes in Landscapes
Planting the Natural Garden
Piet Oudolf Henk Gerritsen
TIMBER PRESS
PIET OUDOLF
HENK GERRITSEN
DRØMMEPLANTER
Aschehoug
Prachtig Gras
MICHAEL KING - PIET OUDOLF
DVA
PIET OUDOLF MEINE LIEBLINGSPFLANZEN
MICHAEL KING
PIET OUDOLF
GARDENING WITH GRASSES
FRANCES LINCOLN
OUDOLF
KINGSBURY
NEUES GARTENDESIGN
MIT STAUDEN UND GRÄSERN
Nieuwe bloemen, nieuwe tuinen
MICHAEL KING · PIET OUDOLF · HENK GERRITSEN
PIET OUDOLF & NOEL KINGSBURY
PLANNEN EN PLANTEN
DUMONT
Michael King · Piet Oudolf
Gräser
Jardins d'avenir
Les plantations dans le temps et dans l'espace
Piet Oudolf et Noel Kingsbury

Sheffield's Department of Landscape who have done some of the most innovative of recent work in researching sustainable planting design. In 2012, they also invited Piet to be a visiting professor. This project is being master-planned by James Corner Field Operations, which invited Piet onto the team. Also on the drawing board is a garden for the new Whitney Museum building in downtown New York to complement the structure being designed by Renzo Piano, and a garden for a well-known American artist.

The Battery

In 2002, Piet was approached by The Battery Conservancy, a volunteer-run association involved in the conservation and enhancement of one of the most historic sites in New York City and one of its oldest public open spaces in continuous use. Dutch settlers installed cannons for defense at the southernmost tip of Manhattan in 1623, to protect what was then the township of Nieuw Amsterdam. By the end of the twentieth century, however, and especially following the economic recession of the 1970s, the 25-acre park had lost its vibrancy. The Conservancy was set up to restore and renew it, in collaboration with the city's Department of Parks & Recreation.

The Battery was a relatively unusual project for Piet in that it called for working within the context of an established and quite traditionally landscaped park. It meant close collaboration with a group of interested amateur enthusiasts who donate their time—and money—to organize, fundraise, plan, and achieve something for the public good. It is led by Warrie Price, who had worked with the U.S. diplomatic service, and who was "mentored by Lady Bird Johnson starting at age eighteen."[1] Volunteers also assist with the park's management, and indeed helped Piet and city workers with the planting. Landscape architects Saratoga Associates worked on the hardscaping. The first phase of development, The Gardens of Remembrance, was completed in 2003 and stands as a memorial to the victims and families of the tragedy of September 11, 2001. Another phase, called The Battery Bosque for the trees that define the site, was completed in 2005. As is often the case, connections made through one job lead to more—involvement with the Battery has led to more work for Piet in New York, through WXY Architecture, who designed the Battery Seaglass project.

Views of The Battery, at the southernmost tip of Manhattan.

UNIQUE ATTRIBUTES

Why has Piet's work as a designer received such acclaim? An attempt to break down what makes his designs unique perhaps comes down to three main factors:

- the reliability and longevity of the species and cultivars in his plant palette,
- attention to plant structure, which provides interest not just in the summer but in the autumn and for much of the winter as well, extending his repertoire of plants beyond the evergreens traditionally relied upon,
- the spatial arrangement of plants is harmonious, coherent, and legible, but also complex enough to hold attention.

Plant Longevity and Reliability

Public plantings must take into account the durability of the species intended for a given space—and private clients of course appreciate designs that incorporate a long lifespan as well. Piet's experience and, to some extent, intuition have helped him accumulate data on plant longevity in a variety of conditions. The repeatedly successful implementation of his palette, which is composed of plants that have a fairly predictable long-term performance, has done much for his credibility as a designer. The mastery of these technical and objective considerations allow his creative vision to flourish.

Horticulturalists and domestic gardeners are often quick to blame less-than-ideal conditions or predators for plant death. These factors of course play a role, but there is also no doubting that a substantial minority of garden "perennials" have a fundamental genetic predisposition toward a short lifespan. Choosing plants for the appropriate environment is of course important, and it is worth bearing in mind that stress, disease, and high fertility can shorten lifespan.

Plant Structure

If a photographer were to take a black-and-white photograph of an Oudolf planting, it would still reveal plenty of character. This is because Piet has always focused first on the structural aspects of plants, as opposed to the color of their blooms. He is not the first to do this, but perhaps he is the first to do so systematically with perennials. The basic vocabulary of structure will be different for different climate zones, so a general discussion of it cannot be applied to all situations. Piet would advise gardeners and designers to look at all the reliable plants that grow in their area and to devise their own structure categories. Once a language of plant structure is decided upon, it can become almost a set of objective criteria for determining what to plant in any given situation.

Agastache nepetoides, a plant favored by Oudolf for its unique structure.

One vital and unique distinction Piet has always made is between structure and filler plants, the latter's role being as sources of short-season color. Structure plants usually account for approximately 70 percent of his planting designs.

Another important aspect of structure that Piet has always stressed is the question of how long a plant's "good" structure might last. In the February 2013 issue of *Gardens Illustrated* magazine, he provided a listing of his "100 Must Have Plants." Within that list, he provided some useful categories, which are worth repeating:

- Short-season and filler plants. These have interest lasting less than three months, or have good foliage but no real structure. Some look untidy after flowering. Many are primarily useful for filling gaps earlier in the year.
- Medium-length season plants. These species retain interest for at least three months, because of foliage structure and seed heads as well as flowers.
- Long-season plants. These include perennials, grasses, and ferns. Their interest endures for at least nine months, because of good foliage structure and seed heads as well as flowers.

Spatial Arrangements

This is the most difficult part of Piet's work to explain, where an artistic eye obviates any need for rules or formulae. As Piet himself says, "other people use the same plants as I do, but their gardens don't look like mine." Intuitive criteria for choosing plants, putting them together, and distributing them across a space cannot be taught or illustrated with a diagram.

The broad leaves of *Hosta* 'Moody Blues.'

The delicate blooms of *Geranium* x *oxonianum* f. *thurstonianum*.

Those who wish to study the methodology behind Piet's plans and plantings may find researching the following factors instructive:

- total number of taxa (species, cultivars)
- the number of genera (some genera may be present as several species or varieties)
- distribution of taxa across the entire planting
- distribution of taxa in smaller units of the planting
- juxtapositions of plant taxa
- location of particular varieties within a planting (e.g. front, middle, back)
- repeated combinations
- linkages between individual clumps of particular plants
- hierarchies of structural dominance and the roles of plants with lower impact (e.g. lower-level linkages between areas)

Perhaps the second most important "hallmark" of Piet's work, other than structure, is repetition. It creates a sense of coherence, it helps make a planting legible, and it can be used to create a sense of rhythm; these three elements together create visual harmony. With enough of a variation in structure, and a wide enough range of structures (i.e. plant taxa), a garden will have contrast, interest, and complexity. When harmony and complexity are in balance, Piet has achieved what he has set out to create.

Oudolf with Warrie Price and head gardener Sigrid Gray at
The Gardens of Remembrance on The Battery in New York in 2002.

Warrie Price originally approached Piet after he won the commission for the Lurie Garden. "I just got on a plane and went over to meet him," she says. "I went to the garden (at Hummelo) and met Piet and Anja. I was struck by his hands—he has huge hands. He is not shy but reserved, shall we say, but once his hands are in the soil he has no reservations. He showed me lots of plants, many his own cultivars." Piet spent a significant amount of time with Warrie, an essential step in building a personal relationship as the base for a project that would clearly last many years, as well as a way for Piet to understand what she and the Conservancy wanted. Warrie recalls how they "went to the Kröller-Müller Museum,[2] partly to look at what he *doesn't* do, but also to gauge my aesthetic reaction to things. We traveled to Enköping too. That was important, seeing another public garden he had designed." Warrie also went to the Floriade in 2002, and credits his design of one of the gardens there with inspiring the look of the Bosque in New York.

Given its closeness to the World Trade Center site and its nature as a memorial, the symbolic value of plants is stressed heavily by the park's guides and interpretive materials. Visitors are encouraged to see living plants as symbols of renewal and rebirth. The park and Conservancy have had their own rebirth of sorts now as well, after Hurricane Sandy's 13-foot (4-meter) storm surge on October, 29, 2012. The park was completely swamped, and another storm the following week further damaged the landscaping. Most of the plants survived the inundation, but many records were lost when the Conservancy's office was flooded.

The Battery attracts enormous numbers of visitors, both native New Yorkers and tourists on their way to the Ellis Island and the Statue of Liberty. With so many of them wanting to know plant names, the Conservancy commissioned a guidebook that points out their locations and provides vital data. It is also one of the world's first to be printed on tear-free, weatherproof, synthetic paper—every garden visitor's dream!

Piet's commission in New York finally convinced his son Pieter that his father was not just hitting a reasonably successful stride in his career, but was actually making a real impact. "Now it all came into perspective," he told me. "I can look back and see all the years and all the work he did with the nursery. He has a knowledge other designers don't have ... if you have both the experience of growing plants and the feeling for good design, you can excel. That is what happened with my father." He remembers that "until the 1990s, he was making money in the summer season, but then the winter would eat it all up. It was stressful at times. When you see all these cars parked on the road next to the garden, you think the plant sales must be going well, but in the end you always have to invest so much to keep it rolling. The last ten years have helped a lot."

By the early 2000s, it was indeed clear that Piet had well and truly arrived. But, inevitably, the special feeling of the "pioneering days" was gone. "There was a special feeling at Hummelo then," remembers Pieter. "You could get plants here you could get nowhere else. There was a special crowd of people. All that changed in 2000, when everyone started selling the same plants. The special feeling never came back—it became mainstream."

The Trentham Estate: An English Labyrinth

Piet met the English landscape designer Tom Stuart-Smith at Chelsea in 2000, when Tom was constructing a garden sponsored by a French wine company. "We met several times as friends, then one day he came to me to ask me to help him at a place in England—Trentham," Piet recalls. That was the birth of what has been a notably successful collaboration, typical of Piet's working method, whereby he has enough discussion to ensure compatibility of vision and a coherent design, but otherwise works by himself. "I was working in a Piet sandwich," Tom recalls. "He was doing a project on either side of the one I was working on." The Trentham Estate is a vast garden designed in the eighteenth century by the fashionable landscape architect Lancelot 'Capability' Brown. At its core, it features a mile-long lake (1.6 kilometers) that was meant to give the grounds a naturalistic effect. The Victorian Era, however, saw the construction of a very formal Italianate Garden.

The earliest days of garden development at Trentham Gardens in Staffordshire.

BLOCK PLANTING

As Stefan Mattson, who commissioned Piet to make Dreampark in Enköping, noted, Dreampark was planted in a series of blocks of more or less equal size, with multiples of the same variety in each block. The plant density in each block varies, depending on the species. The plants-per-square-meter guide Piet had calculated was included in the nursery catalog, which always made it a very useful document to have. This block planting style can be thought of as an ordinary garden bed writ large, and where each individual plant is multiplied in a large clump. Dreampark offered its visitors the chance to walk among big beds of perennials, to lose themselves in a labyrinth-like world of flowers and foliage. Stefan Mattson said he particularly appreciates Dreampark's "mix of wildness and cultivation. What strikes me that it is not wild but it is not a normal planting, either—it's a symbiosis of both."

The current zeitgeist is very much about "intermingling," though the block planting approach, as Stefan agrees, should not be abandoned. Its main advantage is that it is straightforward to manage. It also appears to be immediately and impressively legible, which is an important factor for the public in regions where nature is often granted only a low status. It is also fairly easy to design. Piet continues to use it, either in close combination with other planting schemes or alongside more complex beds.

Over the years, some of the best-loved of Piet's plantings have exploited the feeling that Stefan describes as "losing yourselves in a labyrinth." In these gardens, people are drawn into an area where the plants envelop visitors, creating a separate plant world. This sense of pleasing isolation is created in part by the fact that so many of the traditional props of gardens are lacking: sharply defined borders and large areas of lawn. Pensthorpe and Trentham are similar in many ways in their immersive quality. Winding paths take you through the planting. The entrance to Pensthorpe uses tall perennials to create a portal effect. The Lurie Garden uses short-to-medium-height plants, but has a gently rolling topography that also creates a similar effect, of a self-contained and intimate landscape.

Looking analytically at the distribution of the blocks of plants in these gardens, it is clear that a sense of unity is created through repetition, but the repetition is done with a very light and subtle touch. There is only just enough repetition to continue to remind us that we *have* seen a given plant before, somewhere nearby. Piet manages this by using a considerable number of varieties of plants, a good deal more than most designers would in a garden with the same scale. Trentham

Block planting at Maximilianpark in Hamm, Germany.

features 120 varieties in 70 genera, and Bad Driburg 74 varieties in 44 genera; most larger plantings fall somewhere between these two proportions. In fact, counting frequencies of plant blocks reveals pretty low numbers; in the approximately one-third acre (1,500 square meters) that comprises the Lurie Garden's Light Plate for example, *Stachys officinalis* 'Hummelo' and 'Rosea' occur as a total of eight clumps, *Baptisia* 'Purple Smoke' nine. Frequencies of the blocks of flowering perennials in Pensthorpe's one-acre planting (4,500 square meters) are similar, with nearly all species occurring fewer than ten times, and in many cases fewer than five. The sheer range of species and cultivars creates a truly rich viewing experience, and yet, as we have seen, our senses are not overwhelmed by too rich a set of different visual stimuli.

The Trentham Estate is today run as an upmarket visitor attraction that includes shopping facilities, a restaurant, and an array of activity areas for children. The gardens have played an invaluable role in giving the commercial interest of the estate continuity with its heritage and environment. Tom has replanted the ornate Italian layout with a range of perennials very similar in many ways to that used by Piet, giving an old design a new lease on life. Piet recalls "meeting the developer—that was when [the economy was] good, and he planned all sorts of attractions." Piet's main project here, completed in 2004, consisted of planting a half-hectare (5,500-square-meter area) of perennials, now known as the Floral Labyrinth. It is one of his very informal, immersive plantings. He also designed a unique, stylized meadow about the same size, based on varieties of *Molinia caerulea*, with water-tolerant plants added to take account of occasional flooding. As he explains it, this was very much "a reaction to the environment" planting.

Changes in the Garden at Hummelo

During the mid 2000s, the front garden at Hummelo began to change. By 2005 the ellipses of *Stachys byzantina* and all the lawn turf were taken out and the entire area planted with perennials. Occasional flooding still occurred, which caused the yew columns—so very sensitive to poor drainage—to deteriorate. One by one, they were removed. Originally, when visitors reached the end of the diagonal path across the lawn, they were confronted by what looked like a 165-foot-long (50-meter-long) stretch of perennials and grasses backed by the yew curtains. This perennial planting has stayed substantially the same. Although at first sight it appears to be an impassable expanse of planting, closer exploration reveals a network of three interconnecting circular brick paths. These take visitors on a carefully planned walk through the garden that makes them look at it from many viewpoints: back at where they came from, at plants from different angles, and at the same plant with different foregrounds and backgrounds. It is a sociable kind of space; the paths not only bring people back to the two cross-overs between the three circles, but are narrow enough that they force them to step aside for others—especially those trying to take pictures. Conversation with others visiting the garden is therefore subliminally encouraged. For

Autumn at Hummelo.

visiting groups it is ideal, as they can keep on meeting up with each other and exchanging notes, experiences, and plant names.

At the rear of the nursery area, changes were happening too. The nursery was still popular with visitors, but the pressure to produce plants for Piet's design work was reduced, since more and more wholesale suppliers began to stock the plants that he needed for his palette. Piet's design work was also simply beginning to take up more time, leaving less opportunity for plant selection and breeding. Others in the nursery business, such as Coen Jansen and Hans Kramer, had started to offer a wider and newer plant range. With the importance of the mother plant beds waning and Piet needing more office space, he and Anja made the decision to turn part of this area over to a new building.

Architect Hein Tomesen was commissioned to design a two-story building that would include a commodious studio space for Piet, and accommodation for guests. It was completed in April 2008, and its austere cube form and pale brickwork make it a contemporary contrast to the traditional farmhouse. Around it, Piet planted a new area, which he calls simply "the office garden." Its form is notably much more simple than anything else on the property. *Spodiopogon sibiricus* dominates, with some *Calamagrostis acutiflora* 'Karl Foerster' and *Rhus typhina* whose scarlet-orange leaves in autumn look spectacular against the pale grasses. On the east side there is *Molinia* 'Transparent,' whose leaves make a contrast with the other grasses, and some of that old favorite *Eupatorium maculatum*, but not a lot else. Between the garden and the new studio, the gaps offer a home to the self-sowing grass *Stipa offneri*.

Further International Commissions

A complete contrast was the garden Piet created around this same time for a German client in Bonn, along the banks of the Rhine, which is almost completely sheltered from strong winds. In this scheme, the house was the focal point and the garden was designed as a series of clearly distinct spaces. Here, a variety of plant combinations was employed to reflect and complement the range of ecological habitats created by buildings and trees.

Collecting II

The shelves of Piet's office are populated, not just by books, CDs, and nursery catalogs, but figurines. Usually around 8 inches (20 centimeters) tall, they appear to have walked straight out of the pages of a comic, or a Japanese-inspired manga narrative, or off a grafitti-covered wall of some gritty inner-city neighborhood. These are his collection of "designer toys," sometimes also called "urban vinyl," and are collectors' items of strange characters fresh from the fertile imagination of street art.

First made by Hong Kong artist Michael Lau in the late 1990s, the figures soon caught on, and there are now hundreds available. Piet says that he "used to collect tin toys, back in Haarlem, but then when we moved, I had to sell most of them to raise money for the nursery. Later, when I was travelling in America, I would visit these little comic-book shops, and toys that represented the characters were starting to become available. In Los Angeles, when I visited Robert Israel and we were doing the Lurie Garden together, he took me to some shops where artists were selling their work, including the toys." Every time he travels, Piet now searches for more to add to the collection. "I like the decorative and contemporary aspects of them—they're like street art, part of the urban culture," he says.

As well as pieces by Michael Lau Piet collects figures by KAWS, a New York–based artist and designer; Gary Baseman, an illustrator and animator; and Bounty Hunter, a company based in Harajuku, a neighborhood in Tokyo famous for youth culture and fashion.

S.F.B.B.

Two of Oudolf's later international commissions, a private garden in West Cork, Ireland, top, and Potters Fields in London, below.

A small London park was completed a year later, in 2007: Potters Fields. Located on the south bank of the Thames, it has a view of the Tower Bridge so well known to generations as a symbol of London, as well as the historically important Tower of London. The Greater London Authority employed landscape architects Gross Max to develop the master plan for this new public park. Their principal, Dutchman Eelco Hooftman, brought Piet on and described how he felt that they had "an affinity, so we hardly needed to talk." As with many public, contemporary landscape projects, community participation was encouraged, which required a great deal of talking to local residents, gathering their input about the features they would like to see, and including these into the design. The greatest problem, though, with gardens run by local park staff is maintenance—or rather the lack thereof. Piet insisted that he would only work on the Potters Fields design if it was managed not by the local authority, but by a trust. In the end this was negotiated, and one person became responsible for the site's care and management.

Evolving Ideas

In 2006, Piet and I published our second book together, *Planting Design: Gardens in Time and Space*, with Terra and an English coedition by Timber Press. This book was a joint production, and included my ideas as well as Piet's. We chose the very general theme of "Time and Space" because for us every garden, with the exception perhaps only of very static topiary gardens, is heavily influenced by time. A garden changes—and with it the initial layout or design—so we wanted to explore garden design in the context of what happens as the years tick by.

The book starts by looking at various human reactions to nature, in particular at how gardeners were responding to a growing awareness of ecology as a source of inspiration and information. As part of this examination, we referred to a body of knowledge that has proved remarkably full of insights for gardeners: what has become known as CSR theory (Competitor/Stress-tolerant/Ruderal). This way of looking at plant survival strategies in nature was developed at the University of Sheffield in the 1980s by a team led by J. Philip Grime. I had found it very insightful, as had many practitioners in Germany. Although it has to be said that it is perhaps less useful for those of us who garden in the

mild and wet northwest of Europe (including The Netherlands), where the generous conditions of nature allow us to mix and match plants with abandon in a way almost inconceivable to those in central Europe or most of North America.

It was interesting to examine how time changes gardens. This is an aspect of the process of change ecologists call "succession," and required a discussion in the book of plant lifespans. Finally of course, we had to give some tips for planting practicalities and maintenance.

The question of maintenance can be a sore one. Tom de Witte has accompanied Piet back to some gardens he created years before. "Things are not always as good as they could be," he reported to me. "Maintenance is sometimes a bit of a drama, there are always some problems with invasive plants, but Piet always looks forward." Discovering that one's creations have been neglected or mismanaged is one of the real downsides of working with planting design. It is a situation qualitatively different to that of every other creative profession. What we do is almost inevitably considered temporary. Piet seems phlegmatic in such situations. I have been with him too in places where care has been less than adequate. He will manifest obvious disappointment, but at the same time, it does not appear to get him down. He has learned to master his emotional reactions to things that do not work out the way he has hoped they would, rather than to fight the nature of his profession: plants do not always grow the way we would have liked, clients make changes, storms blow, floods rise, frosts freeze, weeds grow. All gardeners, professional as well as amateur, must accept and deal with undesirable changes. Poor quality or inappropriate maintenance is annoying and disappointing, surely, but in the end it feels almost inevitable, like the weather, another element we cannot control.

BORDERS

The word "border" has a specific and entrenched meaning for gardeners. It defines a particular spatial framework, particularly for British gardeners, where perennials occupy a long, narrow, and rectangular strip with a backdrop—hedge, wall, or fence—behind one side. Borders, in one sense or another, do of course play an overwhelming role in Piet's private gardens, but ever less so as his projects have evolved from medium-sized private gardens to much larger spaces, or projects where the restricted viewpoints needed to appreciate a traditional border are rejected. His borders always have a strong element of repetition, which is vitally important for establishing rhythm and a sense of unity in a linear format. There is always a sense, though, of Piet wanting to liberate himself from the border, and this is particularly apparent at Hummelo, where over the years perennials have moved from merely lining the outer edges of the garden to filling the garden freely from side to side.

The English border has increasingly come to be seen as a clichéd and formulaic way of using plants. I remember Professor Peter Kiermeyer, when he was head of the Sichtungsgarten Weihenstephan, telling me that he thought that viewing such borders was "reviewing soldiers on parade." The strip-like format can also be very limiting to our visual appreciation of plants. Another German, Gabriella Pape, told

The garden at Hummelo.

me that she believed English-style borders stopped us from appreciating the full beauty of grasses because they impeded backlighting, which grasses need to show themselves to full effect. So, in Britain at least, awareness of the Oudolf planting style has gone hand-in-hand with looking at perennial plantings in a much more expansive way.

Inevitably, in the early years of his career, Piet worked with conventional planting spaces in moderately-sized private gardens. Sometimes these are read as old-fashioned containers with new contents, as with a long, narrow town garden—Hesmerg (1993) or the much more dramatically contemporary Boon garden (2000). The Thews garden (1996, 2006) was more innovative in its design, but the spaces filled with perennials were still small. In all of these gardens, the interplay with clipped shrubs made for a jolt to those who expected to see a traditional border next to a lawn or terrace. In the Hesmerg garden, the lawn is held at bay by a repeating pattern of diagonally-oriented box squares. Private gardens are the only Oudolf designs that continue to feature conventionally shaped borders; for example, in one private Haarlem garden (2006), a swimming pool dictates a strong linearity to the rest of the garden but Piet mediates this by installing wonderfully colorful borders that sweep past it and down to the house.

The Boon's private garden in The Netherlands.

The High Line's southernmost point in Autumn, top,
and representatives of Friends of the High Line visiting Hummelo, below.

The High Line

Every now and again, a landscape project is realized that forever changes urban landscape design as a whole. Very often these revolutionary projects do not receive the attention they deserve, or remain as one-off projects that garner the admiration of a few professionals, but do not catch on with the public. The Landschaftspark Duisburg-Nord in Duisburg-Meiderich, Germany, is one. It is a celebration of a vast steelworks—a vestige of Germany's industrial heritage—and is treated almost as a shrine by visiting landscape professionals. Zürich's MFO-Park, a vast steel pergola covered in climbing plants that is equally impressive stays relatively unknown, however.

New York's High Line has been an enormous success with the public and professionals. It has also stimulated interest in creating similar projects all over the world. It was timed well, as the city began to experience a rise in real estate investment that pushed new development into Manhattan's far west side and made the idea of having green space running through a formerly industrial section of town an appealing attribute to the development of a residential area. It also picked up on the interest in gardening and greenery that had been taking hold of the city's residents since the millennium.

It is perhaps useful to think of the High Line as having two design "parents." One is La Promenade Plantée, a 3-mile-long (4.7 kilometers) elevated parkway that runs along the course of an old railway line in Paris, designed by landscape architect Jacques Vergely and built in 1993. The other is the Südgelände, an 18-hectare park in Berlin, which opened symbolically in 1999 as a public space. Its former life was as a railway marshalling yard that was finally abandoned in 1993, and soon thereafter covered over by a rapid growth of birch trees and other spontaneous pioneer vegetation. This created a combination of industrial ruins and nature that many people found singularly attractive. It was, in fact, simply the most talked about of a whole series of post-industrial landscape parks in Germany. Whereas many other countries with an untidy and disintegrating industrial heritage bulldozed it all away and sowed grass on top, as in Britain, Germany generally took a different approach. Ecologists recognized very early on that the vegetation and the wildlife

Views of the High Line before renovation, above, and in late winter 2014, left.

Oudolf with Robert Hammond, cofounder of The Friends of the High Line, at the Venice Biennale in 2010.

infiltrating these sites had a great deal of value. A number of landscape designers and academics became interested too, with the result that there are now quite a number of parks or preserved environments in former industrial areas. These teach visitors to appreciate nature's remarkable ability to heal the scars of dereliction.

Although the U.S. is known for open space and seemingly limitless new horizons for development, its major cities, particularly those in the "Rust Belt," feature plenty of derelict, post-industrial space as well. The High Line was unusual in that it was right in the middle of a major city, and was the last of its elevated rail lines to remain standing. Built in the 1930s to deliver freight to and from the Meatpacking District, it was finally abandoned in the 1960s. The southernmost section was demolished, but the northern section became a remarkable "secret" space that featured a unique, spontaneous flora of native species and garden escapees. It was not supposed to be accessible to the public, and was frequented only by graffiti artists, naturalists, and the makers of art movies. During the 1990s, the administration of Mayor Giuliani proposed its demolition.

A surprisingly strong opposition to the removal of the High Line came from local residents, and in 1999 an action group was formed by Joshua David and Robert Hammond: The Friends of the High Line. The group saw the potential of the High Line to provide public green space in a part of the city where there was very little, and which was then beginning to experience a surge in residential development. Mayor Michael Bloomberg, elected in 2001, headed an administration known for its green initiatives, and as Robert says, "partnering with the city changed everything." Feasibility studies led to the decision to create a public park and a design competition was organized. In 2004 James Corner Field Operations was selected to begin the transformation. Diller Scofidio + Renfro and Piet were invited to join the design team. James Corner is an innovative landscape architect who has made a name for himself by working with artists and photographers and by fearlessly trying to bring a wild spirit into urban landscapes. He is also known as a landscape theorist and writer.

Behind James Corner—and indeed many contemporary U.S. landscape professionals—stood the formidable figure of the Scottish-born Ian

McHarg (1920–2001). He promoted ecological landscape design to students at the University of Pennsylvania in the 1960s and 1970s. He was a trenchant critic of industrial civilization, and an unashamed polemicist who lashed out at what he dubbed the "Dominate and Destroy" ethos of modern humanity. His impact, particularly on his students, was enormous, while his book *Design with Nature*, published in 1969, continues to be highly influential.

The North American landscape profession, now known for being at the forefront of dealing constructively with environmental problems, owes a large debt to McHarg. Without him, there probably could not have been a High Line. Terry Guen, a landscape architect who was a student of McHarg's, believes that his ideas prepared the ground for Piet so that "when he showed up, there was a familiarity with ecological concepts ... we don't have a garden tradition here, so policy and culture had to change."

Piet had been impressed by the richness of the High Line's volunteer vegetation. Unfortunately, none of it could be retained for the final park—the railway bed was seriously decayed and needed total renovation before it could accommodate the public. The visual challenge in creating a planting scheme for the High Line was to evoke what was there before and thus retain its history. It was a challenge quite unlike anything else Piet has had to cope with in his career, but one, which he felt quite confident taking on. His intensive research into North American native plants for the Lurie Garden and growing many of those species in Hummelo helped him feel comfortable with the species he wanted to use.

The High Line's linear path makes it unusual as a park. It has distinct ends, as well as occasional, dead-end "spurs," that provide vistas out over the city, and three tunnels (two through former meatpacking plants, now converted to residential use, and one other under a newly constructed hotel). To James Corner, the park's shape suggested that when walking through it, people should experience a progression of plantings with different characteristics, so that they reveal themselves gradually and merge one into the next, endowing each section of the walk with its own personality. In addition there had to be a conceit of natural and spontaneous vegetation. For the first phase of development, this was done through two broad categories of planting: grassland and young woodland. For the grassland areas—now dubbed the Chelsea Grasslands after the district the High Line traverses—Piet chose not to go with the species found on the High Line before renovation, namely little bluestem (*Schizachyrium scoparium*), which is inclined to be short-lived in some situations and often floppy, but with prairie dropseed (*Sporobolus heterolepis*). As Rick Darke notes, "the *Sporobolus* was known to be good in city environments. It copes with freeze-thaw, and it stays low." Woodland areas featured small tree species and shrubs such as *Cercis canadensis*, and an open and low ground flora. Low grasses or grasslike plants, such as *Carex pensylvanica* were also included to evoke the kind of vegetation that could be found in areas of young woodland on post-industrial sites.

The first bit of track was lifted in April 2006, marking the beginning of the project; three years later the first section, from Gansevoort Street to West 20th Street, opened to an eager and curious public. Success was immediate. The High Line took off not just as a place to go and relax—at once in the city and yet also emotionally outside it—but also as somewhere to stroll up and down and meet friends or perhaps new people. In this, it is a bit like the *paseo* in a Spanish city. Property prices around the High Line immediately soared. Shops and restaurants sprung up along its length. What was once a fairly run-down area took off, attracting "billions of dollars in new economic development," as Robert Hammond notes. There have been critics, needless to say, who complain about gentrification, a "tourist-crammed catwalk," and the loss of the old auto-repair workshops and mom-and-pop cafés that used to fill the streets below, but for vast numbers of New Yorkers and visitors the experience has been nothing but positive. The views and people-watching on the High Line are two of its great attributes, but "it is the planting that makes it successful," as Robert notes.

The second phase, from West 20th Street to West 30th Street, opened in June 2011. A year later the final section, known as the Rail Yards, was saved when it was donated to the city by CSX Transportation. The second section is very different in character to the prairie-like first section, as it is more hemmed in by buildings. Accordingly, it features a higher proportion of trees and shrubs and accompanying forest-floor planting, giving it a distinctly intimate woodland character.

Views of the High Line's Chelsea Thicket, top, and Gansevoort Woodland, below.

"We had all fallen in love with this wild landscape," recalls Robert Hammond. "But you couldn't leave it exactly as it was. You didn't want to freeze it or, when we knew we had to remove it, to replace it exactly. One time I asked Piet if I could call it a 'natural landscape.' He said no, there was nothing natural about it—it is idealized nature." Robert went on to make an analogy with interior design. "It looks natural to the untrained eye—I equate it to a minimalist room. It looks like it was easy to create, but it was actually very difficult. There is a quote from *The Leopard* that I love: 'For things to remain the same, everything must change.' Piet understood that."

Designing landscapes in city environments is, above all, an aesthetic challenge. Most people consider "real" nature too messy for urban environments, as many British local councils found when parts of city parks were turned over to "wildlife areas" in the 1980s and 1990s. People viewed them as untidy and uncared for; spaces seen as unmaintained in turn attract rubbish and crime, and lose political support for their upkeep or even existence. Yet conventional models of horticulture for urban green space are profoundly out of step with the ethos of our times, which is to embrace nature. A middle way is the concept of "enhanced nature," to borrow the term first used by James Hitchmough and Nigel Dunnett in the first academic book on the new planting movement.[3]

The High Line's planting, while it appears to be somewhat wild in comparison to other formal green spaces in the city, such as Central Park, does take a surprising amount of maintenance. "Because it is a very narrow strip, it is all visible. Nothing can be left wild, as in some other places Piet's designed," notes Kyla Dippong, a staff member who has been with the project since it opened. "We have to find a balance; it is quite tricky." Robert Hammond says that, "It is very complicated to maintain. We are all surprised at how well things have done—better than we thought—but one problem is that things are growing too fast." The fact is that the High Line, like the Lurie Garden, is an artificial environment and a roof garden. Its substrate depth ranges from 18 inches (45 centimeters) to less than 10 inches (25 centimeters) under the perennial and grass areas, and to 36 inches (90 centimeters) under areas with trees. "It is a gigantic experiment," as Rick Darke puts it. "There isn't a whole lot of experience growing plants high in the air in the middle

of New York City. The [imported] soil may be too organic, too fertile … and things have rotted."

In what is undoubtedly a challenging set of conditions for "natural-looking" plant life, the high number of diverse species Piet used lends the High Line enormous strength and staying power. Plantings made by designers on this scale are often very species-poor, which makes them very vulnerable to any problems they face, whereas a wide range of species offers the opportunity for species that cope to do well at the expense of those that do not. This process is of course akin to the ecological process that goes on within a natural plant community. As Rick Darke explains, "Plants are being selected that can cope with the conditions," and some help of course from the staff.

Pests and diseases have been a problem and caused one of the park's few real issues—the impact on grass species, especially *Molinia caerulea.* Prairie grasses however have done well. Some species have seeded. "The calamintha is very aggressive," notes Kyla. "We have to keep it at bay. The vernonia sometimes seeds too, but it's easy to spot." As Piet himself has observed, "There is what you call succession—the situation changes from section to section, especially where there are trees." Tree growth has been a lot more rapid than many people expected, which resulted in changes in ground conditions, so in turn the planting had to change somewhat as well.

Since the first phase of the High Line opened, the very best of the region's expertise has been on tap for advice on the second and the third phases and on management. Patrick Cullina, well known for his writing on growing native plant species and a former vice president of horticulture and science at the Brooklyn Botanic Garden, joined the High Line in 2009 as vice president of horticulture and park operations. Rick Darke has advised informally as well.

Maintaining the High Line takes a specially trained eye. "I previously worked at the Battery," Kyla says. "I think that is why they hired me at the High Line. You can either see the aesthetic or you can't—some people don't get it." Each staff member is allocated a zone for which he or she is completely responsible. "Mine is about two blocks long," says Kyla. "There is very little turnover here" she notes. "Once a

Maeve Turner, one of the gardeners at the High Line, performing routine maintenance.

Oudolf with the gardeners of the High Line, above,
and a view of the High Line near Fourteenth Street, below.

gardener gets in here, they don't want to leave. We started with five and then expanded. The old staff participates in the selection process of the new hires."

"I make an annual visit to the High Line," Piet says. "I meet with all the gardeners. We discuss my ideas about how plants should be allowed to develop and what needs to be managed. I listen to their thoughts and ideas, we discuss what should be done, and I always explain my reasoning if I don't think something is a good idea. I am open to anything that evolves, so long as it looks good and there is diversity. But my basic approach is: if it looks good, why change it?"

According to Robert Hammond, the biggest and most intangible impact of the High Line has been "to bring so much attention to landscape and horticulture." It has also shown on a dramatic scale the possibilities of integrating nature-inspired landscape with urban life. Cities across the U.S.—and elsewhere—are now reevaluating areas of abandoned land and seeing in them the potential for creating areas for recreation. Two examples include Philadelphia's Reading Viaduct Rails-to-Trails Project and Chicago's Bloomingdale Trail. The High Line may one day be seen simply as the first of many projects that brought well-designed green space into the heart of cities. Ian McHarg, looking down from his Elysian prairie, should be pleased.

PLANTING IN LAYERS

The growing complexity of Piet's designs could potentially create problems for those charged with their implementation. His concept of breaking down plantings into "layers" facilitates the setting-out process. The layers are developed individually on tracing paper so that they can be seen together or separately, as need be.[4] As a teacher of planting, I find the concept an extremely useful one. Plantings can be broken down into easy-to-define elements; these generally describe very obvious and ecologically sensible growth-form based categories: shrubs, trees, underplanting, and perennials. They can also be used to define design-based categories such as: matrix plants, scatter plants, and block plants. As a design tool, this is a very useful technique and could be adopted and adapted for many different design styles.

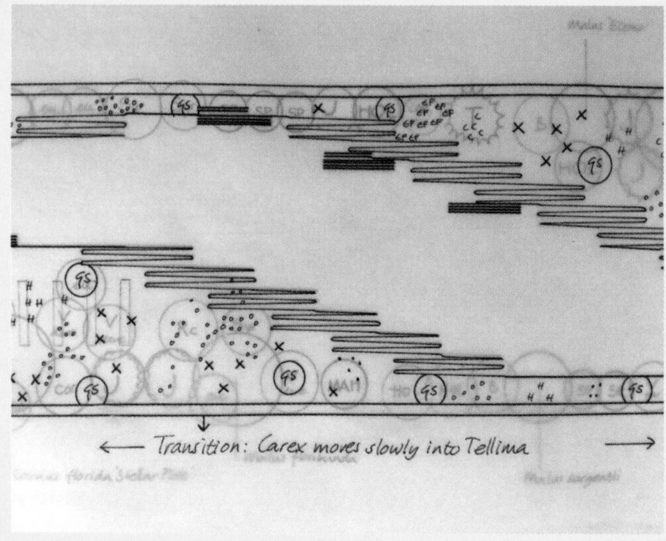

Oudolf often creates plans on tracing paper to demonstrate different layers of plants within a design.

Projects in Germany

The later 2000s found Piet involved in a number of projects for public spaces, or for spaces that were at least publicly accessible. Two such—very different—projects were created in Germany at that time. One was planted in 2008 for the Gräfliche Park in Bad Driburg, a spa town in the northwest of the country. Spa culture became an important part of life in central Europe from the late nineteenth century onward, and spa towns developed a particular look that integrated architecture with carefully groomed landscapes. High-intensity horticulture—usually featuring lively summer bedding—was always an important part of the spa experience. The owners of the spa hotel and park in Bad Driburg, Marcus and Annabelle von Oeynhausen-Sierstorpff, involved Thomas Kellein, an art curator who had secured funding from the regional government to commission installations, sculptures, and other art in open spaces, as part of a project called Garden-Landscape East Westphalia-Lippe. Kellein in turn commissioned Piet to make a planting for the spa's parkland. They requested a contemporary approach to the traditional spa-garden-as-art-form. The spa owners had previously commissioned other notable designers to contribute to the park, including Peter Coats, who created a rose garden; Gilles Clément; and Arabella Lennox-Boyd. Jacqueline van der Kloet was also commissioned to carry out bulb planting. Other people Kellein commissioned for the project included British-Indian sculptor Anish Kapoor, landscape designer Martha Schwartz, and conceptual artist Jenny Holzer.

Piet's part of the Bad Driburg project, which involved 16,000 plants in 80 varieties, was given the distinction of being "freestanding" in the park rather than included to fill in leftover space, as is so often the case with perennial plantings. It is a feature in its own right.

A very different project in Germany, which Piet completed in 2010, was in the gritty landscape of the Ruhrgebiet, a post-industrial zone that had been the powerhouse of German manufacturing from the mid-nineteenth century onward. Germany has handled the transformation of its former industrial areas with considerably more dignity than many other countries; the Ruhr has never become a depressed "rust belt," although there is still no shortage of individual sites that testify to post-

Two German commissions, Bad Driburg in North Rhine-Westphalia, top, and Maximilianpark in Hamm.

industrial dereliction. Landscape regeneration and public art have played a major role in the region's future, and are even being used as part of a strategy to attract tourists. Even the once-grimy industrial city of Essen became a European Capital of Culture in 2010. One of the creations that distinction enabled was a new public park called Berne Park, developed on an old industrial site by landscape architects Davids, Terfrüchte + Partner. Here two concrete tanks, 260 feet (80 meters) in diameter and originally built for industrial water treatment were planted as an art installation, following a design by Gross Max. One became a water garden, the other a sunken perennial garden planted by Piet. The soil supplied was not free of weed roots or seeds, however, so maintaining it has been a struggle.

In 2011 Piet completed another project in northwest Germany: the Maximilianpark in the town of Hamm. The park sits above an old coal mine and is on a former regional garden show site that includes a variety of visitor attractions. The landscaping for the garden was originally constructed in 1984, so it was decided that it could benefit from some contemporary additions.

This period also brought a number of commissions in the city of Rotterdam in the Netherlands, whose old central port quay has long since been made redundant. A 218-yard-long (200-meter-long) series of plantings along the Westerkade (west quay) were designed in a more simple and graphic style than much of his work, so that they could be appreciated at a glance by drivers on the street and joggers and walkers on the pavement running alongside the water. A short walk downstream brings you to Leuvehoofd, where a very different planting guides the eye out to the waterfront, led by a mass of *Deschampsia cespitosa* among groups of perennials.

GRAPHIC STYLING

The graphic quality of perennials in clearly delineated blocks of a single variety can be enhanced greatly by scale, by rigid geometries, or indeed by repetition. Brazilian landscape architect Roberto Burle Marx used these techniques to great effect. Over the years, Piet has also used this approach on a limited number of occasions, and although it is very much a minority aspect of his overall design oeuvre, it can prove useful and appropriate in settings or cultures where a less naturalistic style is favored.

The salvia river in the Dreampark, with its flowing blue and purple massing that runs across a path and toward the river that forms the outer edge of the park, was a dramatic example of this kind of approach. The inhabitants of Chicago are lucky that Piet broke with his normal rule of not repeating his designs to make a bigger version of it in the Lurie Garden as well.

A more formal and geometric example is the planting Piet made in 1996 for the bank ABN AMRO's campus just south of Amsterdam, at Mahlerplein on the Zuidas, which has become the city's new financial hub. It is a rapidly developing area of steel-and-glass high-rise architecture. As Piet describes it, "many people are looking down at the ground from tall buildings, or walking over it on a bridge, so the planting needed to be very graphic." Perennials were laid in monocultural

The Salvia River at the Lurie Garden in Chicago.

The planting at the ABN AMRO headquarters near Amsterdam.

blocks in lines. This project was largely lost during redevelopment, but in 2006 Piet was able to partly recreate it. This chunky, graphic style is not so typical of his work, but it provides ideas and scope for further development in a similar aesthetic.

A number of times, Piet has used grasses to create graphic effects. These attempts have been very successful, particularly when they contrast starkly with flowering perennials. Blocks of grasses have a simple quality, are softly textured, and inject a pale and limited color palette ideal as a restful place for the eye. *Deschampsia cespitosa, Sporobolus heterolepis* (both soft, pale, and fuzzy) or *Molinia caerulea* (with a slightly stiffer feel) have been the main subjects in each case. The Boon garden uses rectangular beds of *Sporobolus* in a wider landscape, where there is the illusion that this grass might be a native invited into the garden. Scampston Hall uses *Molinia caerulea* 'Poul Petersen' to dramatic effect; a part of the garden called Rivers of Grass uses wavy bands of it to alternate with conventional lawn. It looks very different throughout the year, and when seen from a variety of angles. When the viewer is perpendicular to the waves, they read simply as a meadow; when aligned with them, the full shaping effect can be seen. Light and shadow further vary the way the waves are seen. This very simple planting scheme is a dramatic example of the possibilities for ornamental grasses. They can be either starkly contemporary or very formal. The disadvantage of the grass waves is that their effect lasts only part of the year, but for some this drawback is outweighed by the benefit of providing the extra dimension—compared to the traditional formal elements of clipped shrubs—of movement in the slightest breath of air.

Making Connections with Architecture and Art

The late 2000s brought Piet the largest project of his career to date, a 6-hectare planting on the island of Nantucket, near Boston. The owner had bought several adjoining properties, had lifted and moved the houses on them to get the configuration he wanted, and was determined to have Piet design a landscape for the property that could make his vision whole. Piet took some convincing, and confesses to feeling that "it was too big; I felt uncertain." He approached James Corner, his design colleague on the High Line, to take on the master planning of the project.

Nantucket is notoriously windswept, and constant salt spray creates an additional hazard for plants. Trees will not develop to anything approximating their normal size. Piet sought advice from local gardeners and talked with contractors about which trees and shrubs would survive. "They told me nothing would grow taller than about thirteen feet [four meters]. We tried to plant *Cornus kousa*, but it did not work." Among the species that did establish themselves were stewartias, which came as something of a surprise since this relative of the camellia has a reputation for needing sheltered woodland conditions. Piet was also surprised to learn that "Japanese cherries are considered very salt tolerant—you would not expect that. We discovered that sassafras, hollies, and bayberry would also take, so in the end there was actually a lot to choose from." However, he acknowledges that "there were so many unknowns, it was my nightmare." Within the sheltering arms of the wooded areas, Piet next created an extensive series of both perennial blocks and meadow-like pastures where flowering perennials were integrated into a matrix of native grasses.

From 2010 onward, Piet achieved a breakthrough with the architecture and art worlds. For many in the landscape and garden community, this has been of enormous significance. Architects have traditionally rather looked down on landscape designers—the appellation landscape architect to them often translates as "architect manqué." In turn, however, the landscape profession has tended to look down on horticulturists. Gardeners, garden designers—call them what you will—have long battled professional status problems. Even during the eighteenth century, when Britain considered garden-making as a respected field of

MATRIX PLANTING

At the time Piet created the Lurie Garden, it represented a new level of complexity and sophistication in his design. It drew on a number of elements that had proved successful elsewhere, but it also contained several innovations. The bulk of the planting is formed of like plants clumped together, although there is a small area of innovative intermingled planting at the southern end, known as The Meadow, where species are mixed in a truly naturalistic fashion. Its matrix of ornamental grasses, including the native *Sporobolus heterolepis*, is broken at intervals by a number of perennial species that rise up above the grasses; the colors and textures of their foliage and blooms are enhanced by the contrast. This was one of the first times that Piet employed this technique, but it has since become a signature of his style and indeed is on the verge of becoming mainstream in contemporary garden design. He describes it as "my inspiration for most of the High Line."

The word "matrix" is of course derived from the Latin for "mother," so in the context of landscape design, it relates to the idea of a dominant material from which other elements originate. In native landscapes, plant communities often consist of a dominant group of species and a large number of minority elements. For example, meadows and prairies are both grassland communities where around 80 percent of the biomass is grass, while wildflower species make up the bulk of the remaining 20 percent. Matrix planting aims at reproducing this effect, for both aesthetic and practical reasons.

The matrix planting concept appeals to Piet for largely visual reasons, as it allows an area of planting to be created that is easily read as a unified whole, and which acts as a counterpoint to other plants set in it. The first time he used the concept was at Bury Court in 1996, in the Deschampsia Meadow. It was a softly textured area that contrasted gently with the visually strong appearance of the rest of the planting. It was widely copied by both landscape professionals and domestic garden owners, but the original grasses encountered a number of problems and have now been replaced by *Molinia caerulea* 'Poul Petersen.' John Coke also had the idea of planting some *Digitalis ferruginea* and other perennials into it for contrast.

Piet has since found that *Sporobolus heterolepis* gives a similar effect to deschampsia, and is more reliably long-lived;[5] he used it in the Nantucket garden as a matrix for flowering perennials. The deschampsia has however worked well at Leuvehoofd (2012), a quayside planting in Rotterdam. There are good reasons to suppose that there are considerable possibilities for combining cespitose grasses (i.e. grasses that form tight tussocks or bunches) and perennials; in a 1994 article, James Hitchmough made the suggestion that this combination might be a very good way of producing an ornamental but low-maintenance combination.[6] The

A private garden on Nantucket.

High Line is currently the best place to appreciate grass-based matrix planting. Its use of native grass species with (mostly) native perennials that pop up between and through grass plants provides some its most memorable scenery, and effectively evokes the spontaneous vegetation that dotted the railway pre-development. Grasses of the genus *Sesleria* have also appeared as a matrix plant, for example in the Riverside Residence garden in Bonn (2006). Many *Carex* species have potential too, although so far, low and spreading *Carex* species have only been trialed and made commercially available in North America; there are European species that would perform similarly, such as *C. glauca*.

Recent years have seen Piet increase the number of species used to make matrices. Sometimes he uses two or three together—frequently species that are not found forming any kind of matrix in nature. These include cultivars of *Echinacea purpurea* and *Eryngium bourgatii*, often used alongside sporobolus. The perennials can be seen as temporary elements, as eventually the grass will displace them if not managed. The use of plug plants—young perennials, as small as those in 1-inch-wide (25 millimeter) containers grown in bulk quantities—at high densities is another technique that could help create naturalistic or randomised matrix planting. It is being promoted by North Creek Nurseries, out of Pennsylvania.

As with intermingling, Piet's work with the matrix concept is at an early stage of development. More innovation, both from Piet and from those more involved with the technical and ecological aspects of this style of planting, is sure to emerge. For one thing, matrix planting might be a way of "taming" and productively utilizing forceful and even aggressive perennials.

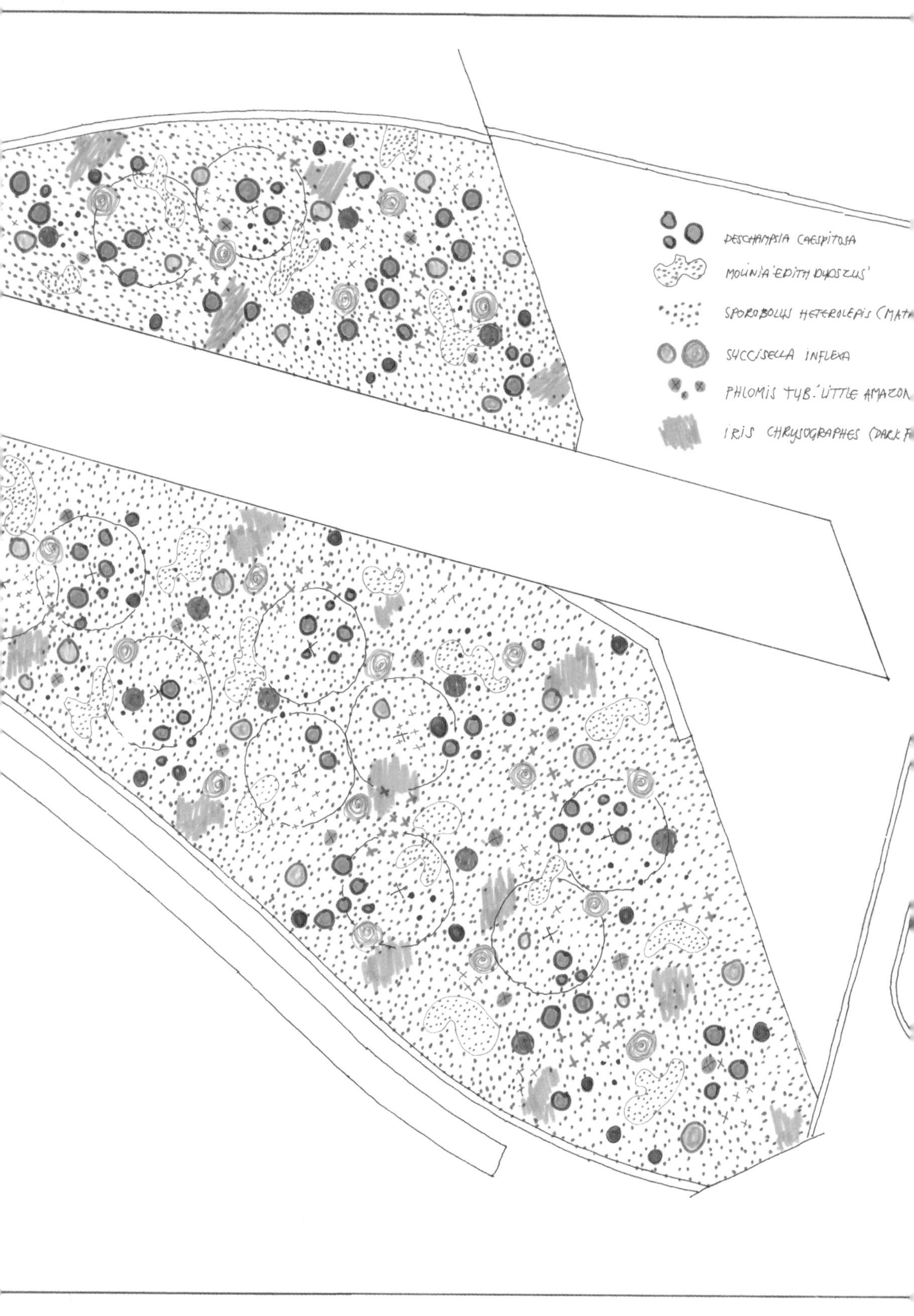
DESCHAMPSIA CAESPITOSA
MOLINIA 'EDITH DUDSZUS'
SPOROBOLUS HETEROLEPIS
SUCCISELLA INFLEXA
PHLOMIS TUB. 'LITTLE
IRIS CHRYSOGRAPHES

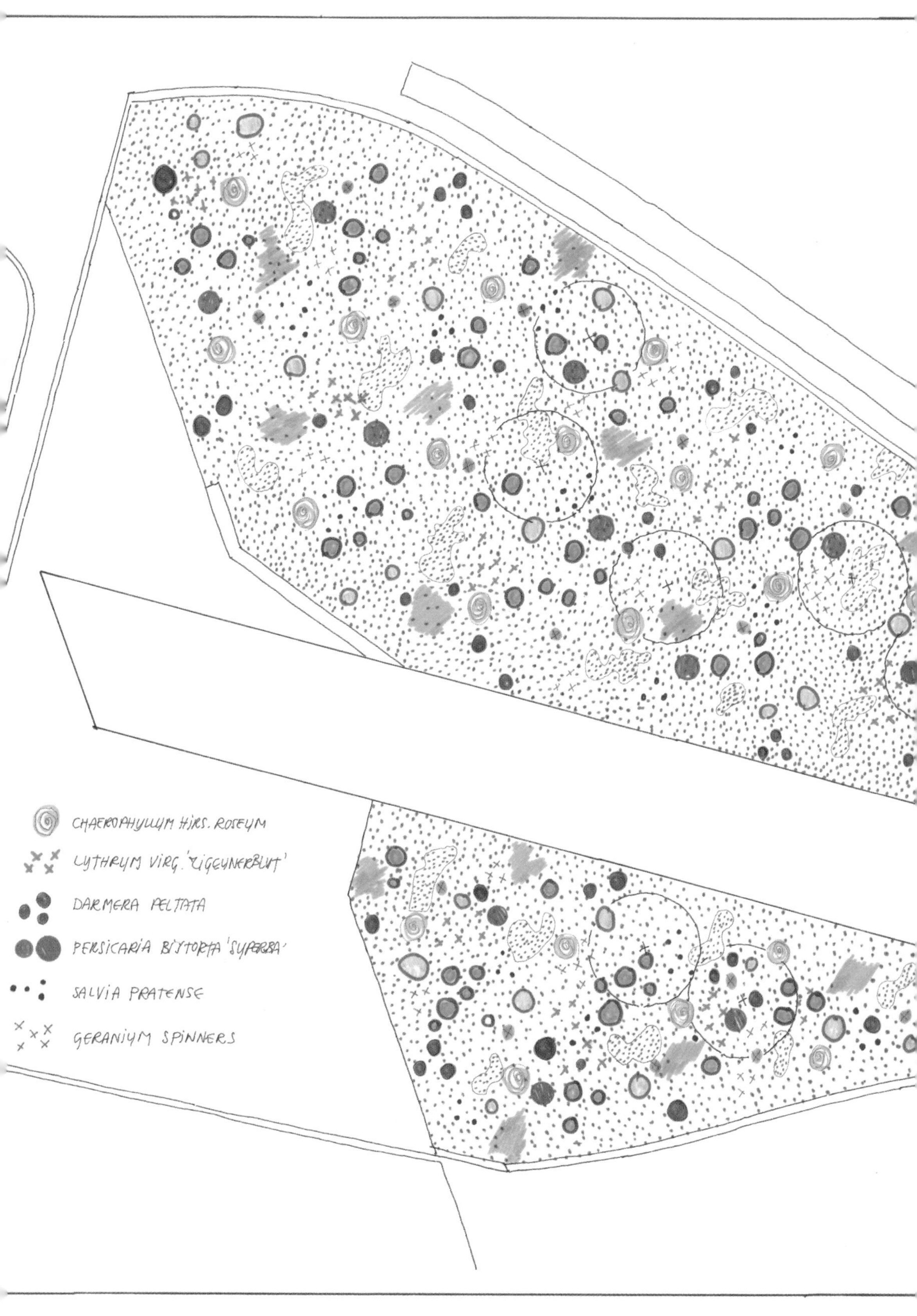
CHAEROPHYLLUM HIRS. ROSEUM
LYTHRUM VIRG. 'ZIGEUNERBLUT'
DARMERA PELTATA
PERSICARIA BISTORTA 'SUPERBA'
SALVIA PRATENSE
GERANIUM SPINNERS

artistry, the actual work of building and maintaining them was regarded as having a very low status. Today, horticulture is often seen only as hobby. Nevertheless, since the 1980s there have been several attempts, in the form of books and public debates, to prove that gardening often has a serious intellectual component. Publications, symposia, magazine articles, and events during the 2000s intensified a discussion that usually revolves around some aspect of this question: Is gardening art?

Landscape professionals have also done an admirable job of showing how their work relates to a larger context, that of "landscape urbanism," or the idea that cities need to be designed as landscapes first, and not as assemblages of commercial buildings constructed out of consideration for profit first and land use second. Many architects have responded positively to this movement, and there has been a great merging of professional interests that allows both types of designers to think more holistically about urban environments. One practical reason for this has been the realization that environmental problems require cross-disciplinary solutions. The rapidly expanding field of green roof creation is a particularly strong example of how architecture, landscape design, and horticulture can come together.

Piet's first breakthrough with the art world came when he was invited to create a temporary installation garden for what is arguably the most important festival of contemporary art, the Venice Biennale. It has been held every other year since 1895. Since 1980, it has alternated with the Architecture Biennale, known as The International Architecture Exhibition. From 2006 onward, it began to cover much more than just buildings—it looked at wider issues of urban planning. The twelfth show, in 2010, was curated by Kazuyo Sejima, one of Japan's leading women architects. She commissioned a garden from Piet to be created in an outdoor part of the exhibition. It was named after the courtyard where it was built, Il Giardino delle Vergini. It was planted amid the remains of historic naval dockyards (the 'Arsenale'), and was intended to evoke a feeling of abandonment.

The following year, a commission arrived from London's Serpentine Gallery. Swiss architect Peter Zumthor had been invited to create the annual summertime architectural pavilion in Hyde Park, and he asked

Oudolf's garden at the 2010 Venice Biennale, above, and the 2011 Serpentine Gallery Pavilion designed by Swiss architect Peter Zumthor in Kensington Gardens, London, overleaf.

Piet to contribute a long, narrow perennial planting to run down a courtyard at the center of his design. Zumthor says, "Enclosed gardens fascinate me. A forerunner of this fascination is my love of the fenced vegetable gardens on farms in the Alps. I love the image of these small rectangles cut out of vast alpine meadows, with the fence keeping the animals out. There is something else that strikes me in this image of a garden fenced off within the larger landscape around it: something small has found sanctuary within something big." Of course, Piet has become known for large-scale and expansive planting—even in small spaces his perennials reach out to wider skies. The Serpentine courtyard invited close and intense examination of individual plants; its design was an invitation to the many visitors to look at plant details up close. Temporary installation-type plantings like this require a very different approach to permanent gardens; they must be made much more dense in order to make an instantaneous impact. It has a near parallel in the creation of a flower show stand. Juxtapositions of plants are tighter, more intense, and more complex.

New Perspectives on Design and Plant Use

The same year, 2011, Piet and I decided that he had created enough new work and generated enough new ideas for us to write a third practical book together, which was eventually published in spring 2013. This book, *Planting: A New Perspective*, relied heavily on his plans to show how intermingling could work. This concept, also referred to as "mixed planting," seemed to us to be very much the zeitgeist in planting design. At its core, it addresses the creation of planting mixtures where multiples of several varieties are combined. Piet had been experimenting with it since around 2000, and it was a major part of the research into planting design that our colleagues in Germany and Switzerland were pursuing. Mixed planting was making headway farther east, in the Czech and Slovak Republics, and the concept was being cautiously tried out by some garden designers in Britain too. Roy Diblik, in Wisconsin, had developed a similar methodology independently, while the British landscape designer Dan Pearson had also created a very interesting blending system of planting—this was only applied in one project, however, the Tokachi Millennium Forest in Hokkaido, Japan.

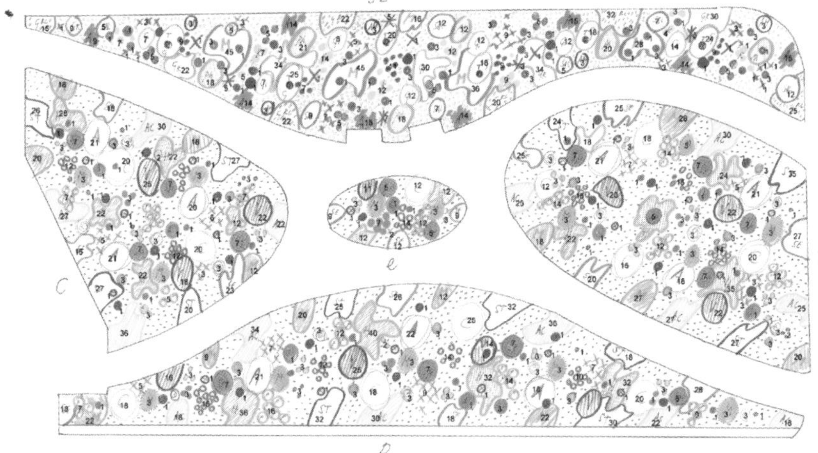

Noel Kingsbury and Piet Oudolf in the 1990s, top, and one of Oudolf's hand-drawn plans for Vallås perennialpark in Halmstad, Sweden, below.

This book also gave us the opportunity to publish some of my research findings into perennial long-term performance, which fit well with a discussion of Piet's work. I had completed a research Ph.D. at the University of Sheffield in 2008, with the title *An investigation into the performance of species in ecologically based ornamental herbaceous vegetation, with particular reference to competition in productive environments.* Basically, I had been trying to apply the lessons of plant ecology science to perennial plantings in order to understand how we could better specify plant selection to commercial users of perennials. One of the problems of doctoral research is that so much time is spent thrashing around trying to find research questions, only to discover that you have not asked the right questions—in short, I wish I knew at the beginning what I realized at the end I did not know and needed to find out. Fortunately, in 2009 I was able to join a European Union–funded research project in which Sheffield was a partner. The overall subject was cost-effective best practices for public space management, so my paper entitled *Evaluating the Long-Term Performance of Ornamental Herbaceous Plants Using a Questionnaire-Based Practitioner Survey* was very appropriate. It tied up a lot of loose ends, and confirmed and clarified many questions I had raised in my thesis. I interviewed nearly seventy gardeners (mostly amateurs) on the performance of some common garden perennials. In some cases, they had decades of experience—two were even in their nineties.

With my research behind me, I began to appreciate the simple, scientific reason for Piet's success as a designer: his plants survive. I remember a conversation with Tom Stuart-Smith in which he expressed what was almost astonishment at how well Piet's plantings lasted. To be able to create a beautiful garden is one thing; to have most of it still flourishing ten years later with very little replanting is another. Piet's experience as a nurseryman and his continued focus on plant longevity are the keys to his design. My research, I believe, complemented his knowledge by providing our readers with useful explanations of plant form, growth over time, physiology, etc. I believe that a better knowledge of the relationships between plant form and performance is crucial to making predictions about the performance of unfamiliar plants.

Acclaim

On September 27, 2012 it was announced that the leading British architects' organization, the Royal Institute of British Architects, had awarded an honorary fellowship to Piet. He is one of the few landscape professionals—and the only designer to work primarily with plants—to be so honored. The organization's citation for these fellowships states that they are awarded to those who "have made a particular contribution to architecture in its broadest sense," including "building more sustainable communities and [educating] future generations."

In 2013, Piet was given the premier Dutch cultural award, the Prince Bernhard Culture Fund. That award goes to "individuals or institutions that have made exceptional contributions in the field of music, theater, dance, visual arts, history, literature, heritage, cultural or nature conservation." The citation noted his "achievements in the field of gardening and landscape design," particularly his "significant impact on developments in The Netherlands and abroad." The award ceremony was held at the Muziekgebouw aan 't IJ, a modern concert hall on Amsterdam's waterfront, on October 11. Piet had been advised that the ceremony would last an hour, but he "wanted it to be a surprise" so he did not get involved in the details of the agenda. Speeches were made; a variety of artists played music—including a band that played Leonard Cohen numbers (a favorite performer of Piet's); a woman read out a list of Latin plant names while photographs from *Landscapes in Landscapes*, the 2011 monograph on twenty-three of his gardens, were projected across the central floor area up on to a huge screen; dancers performed to some hip-hop music that had been selected from Piet's iPad; and finally Queen Maxima gave him the award.

The award includes a prize for Piet himself, as well as an award for the winner to spend for public benefit. Piet is working to establish a fund called "Green in the Neighborhood," which would donate money to community-based and volunteer projects in urban areas. These could include temporary projects, like seed-based plantings to cover sites waiting for development, pocket parks, or vegetable patches. Piet would approve funding in collaboration with a committee from the foundation.

The nursery area at Hummelo, with Oudolf's recently constructed studio building in the background.

Hummelo: Beyond Design

In autumn 2010, Piet and Anja decided to close the nursery at Hummelo. It had begun to seem increasingly superfluous. Its original function had been to supply plants for design work, but now that Piet's success as a designer had stimulated so many of the wholesale nurseries to grow his kind of plants, it was no longer really necessary for them to grow plants themselves. Other nurseries in the country and an increasing number in Germany, Belgium, Britain, and France had also taken over the role of providing difficult-to-find, cutting-edge plants. Many of the Oudolfs' garden visitors also arrived in organized groups, and they tended to buy few plants, often none. Anja felt that her time would be better spent concentrating on organizing and hosting the increasing number of these group visits—Hummelo was now very much on a circuit of organized tours of Dutch and Northern European gardens.

The removal of the nursery provided Piet with a large, empty plot of land. I have a clear memory of arriving to stay the weekend sometime in April 2011; spring sunshine beat down on the ground where the standing-out area of the nursery had been. That weekend, Piet planted out about two dozen *Calamagrostis* 'Karl Foerster.' When I next visited, that autumn, the entire area had been transformed into a kind of meadow with a variety of late-flowering perennials dotted amongst grass. The perennials had been planted, and the "grass" was actually the result of sowing a native wildflower meadow seed mix. Piet said he wanted to create something low maintenance, and wilder than anything he had done before. It was randomization to the point of going beyond design altogether.

Although it looked good, I couldn't help but wonder how long the perennials would survive the grass competition. The ideal of creating a kind of "super meadow" with ornamental perennials growing out of wildflowers and grass has been around a long time, certainly since William Robinson wrote his inspirational and polemical—but mostly theoretical—book *The Wild Garden* in 1870. Quite a few people, myself included, had tried to create one and found that the climate of northwest Europe, with its constant moisture and long growing season, led the wild grasses to grow so well they would eventually smother the perennials. James Hitchmough had run formal trials on such meadows in both

Scotland and northern England, and essentially concluded they were not worth the effort, as so few perennials could coexist with the grasses.

Three years later however, it has become clear that Piet's perennial meadow is a resounding success. For those of us who had put a lot of effort into trying to make this style of planting work, it was humbling and almost embarrassing. The perennials have all formed good clumps and flower well, although at a shorter height than they would do in more cultivated circumstances. The grass-and-wildflower mix has formed a dense sward, but with a relatively low grass proportion. In fact a lot of it is yarrow (*Achillea millefolium*). It is very biodiverse—even simply as a wildflower meadow, it would be admirable.

I rather assumed that the meadow's sandy appearance accounted for light and poor soil to a considerable depth. Apparently not, although the answer may still lie in the soil; Ken Thompson, an ecologist at the University of Sheffield who has written extensively on biodiversity in the garden, maintains that a low phosphorus content in the soil seems to correlate to wildflower diversity. Nitrogen, the nutrient usually blamed for overly lush grass, can be lost quite quickly from soil, but not phosphorus. The perennial meadow is a triumph and a statement. Piet's planting approach, which began with architecturally-driven geometries and has developed incrementally and gradually toward an increasing wildness, is now exploring what feels like an ultimate synthesis of culture and nature. How to create that, Piet reminded me, was the subject of "those discussions with Rob Leopold and Henk Gerritsen, all those years ago."

This latest development in the garden at Hummelo is perhaps a harbinger of things to come. Piet has begun to experiment with making seed mixes from native species supplied by Cruydt-Hoek, Rob Leopold's old business. Seed-sown plantings have risen dramatically in popularity since people were exposed to the spectacular plantings created for the Olympic Park in London. The body of research behind why they work has been led by James Hitchmough.

What I did not know on that visit was that one of the most strongly "cultural" aspects of the garden at Hummelo was about to disappear. Over the years, Piet and Anja's garden has been featured innumerable times in magazine articles and books. Photographers and readers love

A garden at the Hauser & Wirth gallery in Somerset, England, relies on nontraditional paths to give visitors different perspectives on the planting.

the perennials, the grasses, and the seed heads, but they can't keep their cameras away from the curtain of yew hedges at the rear of the front garden. After a while, this innovative, simple, and theatrical element had begun to become something of a cliché.

Flooding and the root death and fungal infections that follow it had also taken a heavy toll on the yew blocks. In August 2010, the area was flooded with almost 8 inches (20 centimeters) of water; waterlogging can often cause more problems for plants in the growing season than when they are dormant in winter. By the autumn, the yew was beginning to go brown, so in May 2011, Piet brought in a contractor with a chipper-shredder and removed them all. Piet had accepted that they had become tired, and was all too aware of them being copied too often—and often poorly. The garden does look very different without them, somehow a little more like an English sunken garden. It appears to be a more self-enclosed and more inward-looking world. I miss those hedges, but at the same time I can see now that they had perhaps become a bit of a distraction. Now, the focus is clearly on the perennials.

The disappearance of the hedges did not sit well with everyone. "One day, two people were walking around our property," Piet remembers. "They were walking back and forth, and I noticed they were not looking at the planting. I went over and asked them if I could help them find something. They said they had come all the way from Brussels to look at the hedges they had seen in the book *Landscapes in Landscapes*. I told them they died, but that there were plenty of other things to see. They were shocked and disappointed. They had driven two and a half hours to see the hedges. Without looking around any further, they got in their car and drove away."

I ran a blog posting about the loss of the hedges. On the whole, people who responded were positive, responding with such comments as: "Change is good." "The only thing that hedges do are make gardens look more English, which is great if that's what you're going for. For the rest of us, any major departure from hedge-dom is good." "Change is good. It brings anguish, anxiety and opportunity. Piet is my hero."[7]

Perhaps that is a good note on which to end our story. Piet has worked so diligently that now someone who designs gardens and public spaces can be called a hero. Now that is progress, and progress of a very good kind.

Piet and Anja circa 1996, above, and Anja with Poppy, below.

HUMMELO, THE BEGINNING

1. *Stinze* plants are non-natives that have naturalized in a benign fashion—many are bulbs.
2. The names mean something different in each language; the Dutch translates roughly to "up the garden path," the German "in neighbors' gardens."
3. Quoted in *Ernst Pagels, aus seinem Leben und Wirken*, Freundekreis uns Stiftung Pagels Bürgergarten, 2013, p. 6.
4. Now Plant Heritage.

BECOMING KNOWN

1. Jean Sambrook, "Visit to Holland Friday September 25th to Sunday 27th, 1987," in *Hardy Plant Society Newsletter*, 1987.
2. Now the Weihenstephan-Triesdorf University of Applied Sciences.
3. 'Geordie' refers to the northwest of England: Northumberland, County Durham. The local accent and dialect are heavily influenced by Norwegian, a legacy of Viking rule a millennium ago.
4. From Charles Quest-Ritson, "Trentham Gardens," in *Garden Design Journal*, Society of Garden Designers, 2008.
5. http://www.lbp.org.uk/downloads/Publications/Management/making-contracts-work-for-wildlife.pdf
6. Now Pensthorpe Nature Reserve.
7. "Mixed planting" refers to a planting style developed in Germany and Switzerland around 2000, which aims to simplify larger plantings through the use of randomized mixes. The mixes have mostly been designed and trialed by technical universities.

CROSSING THE ATLANTIC

1. This former First Lady was the most influential voice in the use of native wildflowers in public landscapes during the 1970s. The Lady Bird Johnson Wildflower Center at the University of Texas at Austin was founded in 1982 "to increase the sustainable use and conservation of native wildflowers,

plants and landscapes," and its Land Restoration Program actively works to apply ecological knowledge to healing damaged areas.

2. A major and innovative contemporary art museum near Hummelo; it is known for its sculpture garden.
3. Nigel Dunnet and James Hitchmough, eds., *The Dynamic Landscape*, Spon Press, 2004.
4. Layering is discussed in detail in *Planting: A New Perspective.*
5. The problems with *Deschampsia cespitosa* are essentially that it tends to be short-lived on fertile soils, and that commercial cultivars are often prone to disease; in suitable environments a genetically varied population of this species does have potential.
6. James Hitchmough, "The Wild Garden Revisited," in *Landscape Design*, May 1994.
7. Quotations taken from comments on "Susan in the Pink Hat" and "Catmint."

ACKNOWLEDGMENTS

Anja and I would like to thank all those who have supported us, believed in us, and inspired us through the years, especially:

Friends and colleagues from the early days, some of whom are regrettably no longer with us.

Fellow growers, plant people, landscape architects, and architects.

Clients, patrons, directors of horticulture, head gardeners, and gardeners.

Those with whom I have collaborated on education.

Journalists and photographers who have followed and supported our work from the very beginning.

And finally, the people who were always there to help us in the garden and former nursery in Hummelo.

Piet Oudolf

Writing this book has of course been a collaboration with Piet himself, whose memory and papers have been scoured for information, stories, plant names, and annoying things like dates. I have also talked to Anja and to Pieter Oudolf, in particular regarding the early days at Hummelo, and also about this period to Joyce Huisman, a family friend of long standing.

I arrived on the scene in 1994, after the pioneering days, but when Piet, and others, were still trying to establish the credibility of his new style of planting. It has been a special pleasure revisiting those days and talking to old friends and contacts such as Fleur van Zonneveld, Leo den Dulk, Willy Leufgen and Marianne van Lier, Stefan Mattson, Eva Gustavsson, and Eugénie van Weede. I particularly enjoyed some reminiscing with John Coke, who provided Piet with his first British commission, and with Rosie Atkins, who played such a crucial role in launching Piet in the English-speaking world through the marvellous and brave *Gardens Illustrated* magazine—its current editor, Juliet Roberts, continues to support Piet's work and that of other innovative designers and plantspeople.

Over the years since then, I have met and corresponded with several other Dutch and German plant people about Piet and the new planting: Coen

Jansen, Brian Kabbes, Wiert Nieumann, Klaus Thews, Hans Kramer, and Eelco Hooftmann. Stane Sušnik I met at Hummelo, and I've always enjoyed getting his unique Slovene perspective. Hélène Lesger I clearly remember meeting first at Hummelo—she was then Piet and Henk's publisher, and has since acted as our agent; she is always a delight to work with and also of course a source of information on the Oudolf story in her own right.

Piet's work has been built in part on the German garden heritage; thanks to Dieter Heinrichs for providing some information on one of Piet's main German links, Ernst Pagels, and also to Michael King for some good stories about Pagels. I have also enjoyed discussing Piet's work with Germany's current leading garden innovator, Cassian Schmidt.

Over in the U.S., I have had several conversations about Piet's work and American experience over the years with Colleen Lockovitch, Rick Darke, Terry Guen, and Roy Diblik, and specifically for this book with Warrie Price, Robert Hammond, and Kyla Dippong. Jennifer Davit, the horticulture director at the Lurie Garden, has contributed a unique insight into the post-planting liaison process with Piet.

Back home my wife, Jo Eliot, has been a great support, as always. I'm also very grateful to a number of people I roped in to help analyze some of Piet's plans: Colin McBeath and Elliott Forsyth in Scotland and Adam Woodruff in St. Louis. I am particularly grateful to Catherine Janson for reading through draft copies and commenting.

Finally, I need to thank those who are no longer with us for the insights into the Hummelo story: the late and much missed Henk Gerritsen, Rob Leopold, and James van Sweden.

Noel Kingsbury

PHOTOGRAPHY CREDITS

Photography by Piet Oudolf, except for the following images:

Battery Conservancy, The: 282-85
Buhler, Karl: 22, 36
Carlson, Robin J., for Lurie Garden: 234, 243 top, 244-53
Checketts, Imogen: 194-95
Edwards, Heather Flower Photography: 374-77 top left, 378-79
Folling, Marianne Photography: 158-59
Gemeente Amstelveen: 15
Henk Gerritsen Foundation: 47, 48-49
Herfst, Walter: 148, 196 top and below, 344 top, 358-59
Hesmerg, Erik Fotografie: 83 top, 210-11
Kleine Plantage, De: 54 top
Maximilianpark Hamm, Bruse Frank: 297
Piper, Thomas: 372 top
Stichting Tuinen Mien Ruys: 43, 44
Swart, Siebe Fotografie: 304-5

THE NETHERLANDS

Leuvehoofd, Rotterdam (2010)

Ichtushof, Rotterdam (2010)

Westerkade, Rotterdam (2010)

De Vlinderhof, Maximapark, Leidsche Rijn (2014)

Groot Vijversburg, Leeuwarden (Planted in 2014)

GERMANY

Gräflicher Park, Bad Driburg (2009)

Berne Park, Bottrop (2010)

Maximilian Park, Hamm (2011)

SWEDEN

Drömparken, Enköping (1996)

Harbour promenade, Sölvesborg (2009)

Public park in Skärholmen, south-west Stockholm (2011)

Juvelen, Jungfrun, and Vallås park, Halmstad (2014)

ENGLAND

Pensthorpe, Fakenham, Norfolk (2000, revised in 2009)

Scampston Hall, North Yorkshire (2000)

Trentham Estate, Stoke-on-Trent (2005)

Potters Fields Park, London (2007)

South Plaza of the Queen Elizabeth Olympic Park, London (2014)

Hauser & Wirth Somerset, Bruton (2014)

CANADA

Entrance of the botanical garden, Toronto (2006)

U.S.

New York

Gardens of Remembrance, the Bosque (2003-2005), and Bikeway gardens (2011-2014), The Battery, Manhattan

High Line, Manhattan (2009)

Goldman Sachs Headquarters, West Street, Manhattan (2009)

Chicago

Lurie Garden, Millennium Park, Chicago (2001)

INDEX